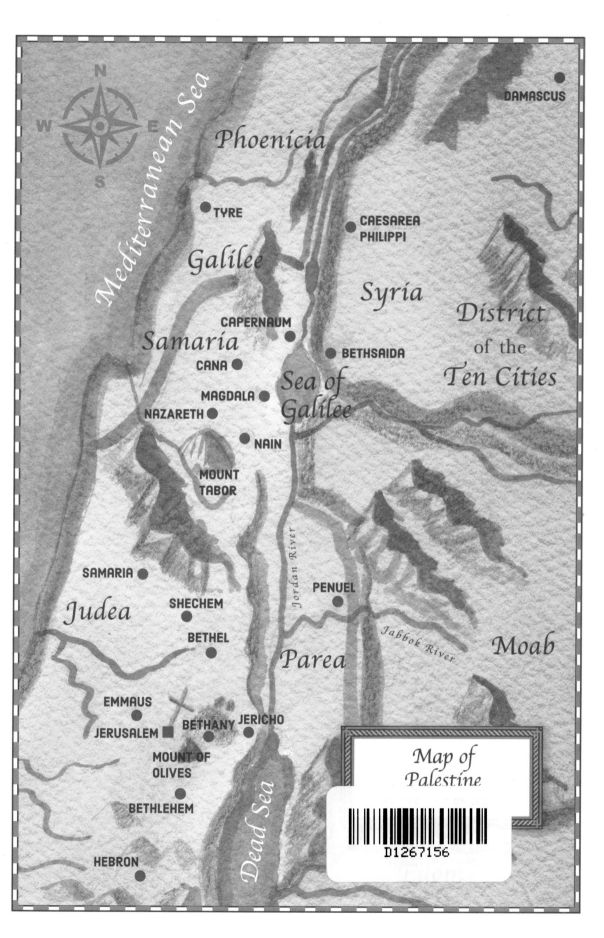

Map of Palestine

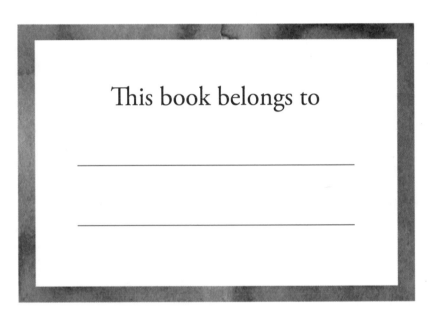

This book belongs to

_____

_____

BOOK *of* BIBLE STORIES

60 SCRIPTURE STORIES EVERY CATHOLIC CHILD SHOULD KNOW

AMY WELBORN

LOYOLAPRESS.
A JESUIT MINISTRY

Chicago

MORE FROM LOYOLA KIDS

LOYOLA KIDS BOOK OF HEROES
BY AMY WELBORN

LOYOLA KIDS BOOK OF SAINTS
BY AMY WELBORN

LOYOLA KIDS BOOK OF EVERYDAY PRAYERS
BY CATHERINE ODELL
AND MARGARET SAVITSKAS

LOYOLA PRESS.
A JESUIT MINISTRY

3441 N. Ashland Avenue
Chicago, Illinois 60657
(800) 621-1008
www.loyolapress.com

Scripture texts in this work are taken from the *New American Bible, revised edition* © 2010, 1991, 1986, 1970 Confraternity of Christian Doctrine, Washington, D.C. and are used by permission of the copyright owner. All Rights Reserved. No part of the *New American Bible* may be reproduced in any form without permission in writing from the copyright owner.

Text of the Magnificat on pages 19–20 is taken from the *New Revised Standard Version Bible: Catholic Edition*, copyright © 1993 and 1989 by the Division of Christian Education of the National Council of the Churches of Christ in the U.S.A. Used by permission. All rights reserved.

Cover and interior illustrations: Laura Michell.

ISBN: 978-0-8294-4539-8
Library of Congress Control Number: 2017942228

Printed in the United States of America.
17 18 19 20 21 22 23 24 25 26 27 Bang 10 9 8 7 6 5 4 3 2 1

LOYOLA KIDS

BOOK *of* BIBLE STORIES

60 SCRIPTURE STORIES EVERY CATHOLIC CHILD SHOULD KNOW

AMY WELBORN

Contents

Introduction

Advent

Christmas

Ordinary Time

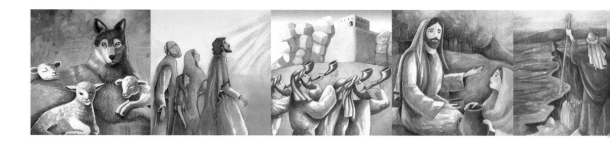

Lent

Easter

Introduction

Bringing Bible Stories to Our Children

On the one hand, we have a child. Perhaps the child is in our family, is a neighbor, or sits in a class we're teaching.

And on the other hand, we have a Bible.

We know that the child and the Bible should meet. We'd like the child to take up that Bible and make it a part of her life. But how? Where do we begin?

The Bible is long, complex, and daunting. There's not much time in our day or our class. How do we include the Bible in a way that's appropriate, not intimidating, and helpful? How do we present the Bible in a way that plants the seeds for a lifelong relationship between that child and the Scriptures?

As the *Catechism of the Catholic Church* explains, God has revealed himself to the world in a Word. That Word is made flesh in Jesus Christ, and that Word is contained in the Sacred Scriptures. It is God's self-revelation. God is the author of the Scriptures.

This means that the Scriptures are inspired by the Holy Spirit. The Holy Spirit's inspiration protects the human authors of the books of the Bible from writing anything but the truth. When we approach the Scriptures, we're confident, because we know we are being given the truth about who God is, who we are, and how God interacts with us.

This means that sharing the Scriptures with children is one of the most important gifts we can give them. We know that each of the children in our care has been created by God and is being called to live in close relationship with God, now and in eternity. It's a lot harder for our children to do that if they can't recognize God's voice in their hearts. We lay the groundwork for that relationship by introducing them to God's voice, speaking his Word, in the Bible.

From the time of the Apostles, Christians have understood that God's Word isn't just a gift to each of us as individuals. It's a gift to us as members of God's people: the Body of Christ.

The most authentic and fruitful way to read the Bible is with that in mind. As the *Catechism* helps us see, when we read the Bible, we remember three basic points:

We're attentive to the unity of Scripture. We don't read verses in isolation or as proof texts. All the books of the Bible come from the unified heart of God, and all are related.

We read the Scriptures within the Living Tradition of the whole Church. Jesus promised that the Holy Spirit would be with the Church always. The Holy Spirit, through the practices, teachings, and prayers of the Church through history, informs our reading of the Bible.

We read with the Creed in mind. The truths taught by the Body of Christ are reflected in Scripture, and the Scriptures are reflected in the Church's teaching.

The stories in this book are presented with these principles in mind.

The Bible in the Life of the Church

Sometimes Catholics are unfavorably compared to other Christians because we seem uninformed about the Bible. This is perhaps true in some ways, but you might be surprised at how great a role the Bible already plays in your life and the lives of the children in your care.

When we go to Mass, we are immersed in the Scriptures. First, there are the Bible readings themselves: four on Sundays, including the psalm, and three for each day of the week.

When you go to Mass on Sundays, you're already being touched by four passages from the Scriptures, all from different parts of the Bible.

Beyond that, many of the prayers of the Mass are rooted in Scripture. The greetings we exchange with the celebrant are echoes of Paul's greetings in his letters and of Jewish blessings. When we sing the *Gloria*, we're repeating the angel's chorus from the Gospel of Luke. When we sing the *Sanctus* or *Holy, Holy, Holy* before the Eucharistic Prayer, we're singing Isaiah 6:3; Psalm 118:26—and what the pilgrims sang to Jesus on his entrance into Jerusalem. We pray the Lord's Prayer, as Jesus presented it in the Gospel account. We pray to Jesus as the Lamb of God, echoing John the Baptist's recognition of Jesus. And, like the Roman centurion from the Gospels, we pray, before receiving the Eucharist, that we are not worthy for Jesus to enter under our roof.

Perhaps you are familiar with the daily prayer of the Church, called the Divine Office or Daily Prayer. Several times a day, from morning to night, Catholics around the world set aside time to praise God. Men and women in religious orders are required to pray these prayers, but many laypersons do as well; the prayers can be purchased in books or found online. These prayers are almost totally composed of passages from the Bible, primarily the Psalms.

So, every day, around the clock and around the world, Catholics are praying from the Bible.

Even aside from the Mass—and if we can't work the Office into our schedules—many Catholics use the Bible as an inspiration for prayer. We might use the readings for daily Mass. We might pick a book of the Bible to read through during the week or month. We might decide to make reading the Bible and praying with it part of an Advent or Lenten devotion. We can do this as adults, and we can do it easily with our children.

This book is intended to help you do just that.

How to Use This Book

When contemplating the content and shape of a book of Bible stories for Catholic children, I asked some basic questions. What would make this book unique? How did I hope this book would help parents, catechists, and children bring God's Word more deeply into their lives?

These Bible stories are presented to children in the context in which most of them heard them first and continue to hear them most frequently: the Mass. The stories in this book are the same stories children and adults will hear in Scripture readings at Mass.

The stories are arranged according to the time of the liturgical year they are most likely to be encountered. Thus, we have stories of the Church seasons: Advent, Christmas, Ordinary Time, Lent, and Easter.

The stories themselves are retold with an eye on the themes of that liturgical season as well as various aspects of Catholic life that are informed by that Scripture passage: prayers, devotions, sacraments, teachings, and the lives of the saints.

A book featuring sixty stories is not comprehensive. It's not intended to replace reading the Scriptures at home or in the classroom. We hope these stories inspire readers to go back and read the Mass readings. We also intend that readers return to the stories in this book and see how they relate to the bigger story of the Church.

Use this book however you like. The stories can be used as an added family or classroom devotion during a liturgical season. They can be used outside a specific season and read and enjoyed on their own. We hope you will enjoy this book with a Bible at your side for deeper reading and exploration. Direct quotes from the Bible appear in purple so that young readers can become familiar with Scripture quotations in the context of the larger story. Each story includes references to where the story is found in Scripture.

I hope you'll see this book as part of a conversation between God and his people that is as old as creation—and a conversation in which you and the children in your care have a part. This is a conversation that we hear in the life of the Church through history, and it echoes in each person's heart, no matter how young he or she is. This sacred conversation begins with God breathing over the waters, and God's voice speaking us into life. It ends, someday, after a life of listening to that Voice, with an *Amen* from ours.

Calendar of the Christian Year

Advent

Prophets Say That a Messiah Is Coming

When we read the stories about people in the Bible, we can learn about our own lives. The Bible tells the story of us humans, beginning with our first parents in Genesis. And it follows our journey over hundreds of years. Sometimes very sad things happened. Sometimes God's people were conquered by other nations. Sometimes these other nations took God's people away from the home God had given them, which was called the Promised Land. When these bad things happened to the people, they wondered, *Why are we suffering? When will God help us?*

During those hard times, certain people would step forward to share hope and good news from God. Those people were prophets. A prophet lives in close communion with God, and so the prophet can teach the people and lead them. A prophet helps people understand what they have done wrong. He shows them when they are going the wrong way, walking away from God. A prophet helps the people understand that God made them and loves them. A prophet teaches people to listen to God. A prophet gives people hope.

One of the greatest prophets was Isaiah. The messages God gave Isaiah to share with the people are contained in the book of the Bible named after him. Isaiah lived in a time of great trouble for God's people. Other nations wanted to take over the Promised Land, and the people did not know what God wanted them to do about it. Isaiah listened to God and helped the people understand.

During hard times, certain people stepped forward to share hope and good news.

Isaiah said there would be a time when all our sins are forgiven—when we will feel and know how close God is to us. This is such good news!

In a vision, Isaiah saw God ruling the world from a holy mountain. He saw all people of the world going toward that mountain—not just the people of Israel, but all other nations too.

> Every valley shall be lifted up,
>   every mountain and hill made low;
> The rugged land shall be a plain,
>   the rough country, a broad valley.
> Then the glory of the LORD shall be revealed,
>   and all flesh shall see it together;
>   for the mouth of the LORD has spoken.
>   (Isaiah 40:4–5)

In this vision, high places are made flat, and valleys are raised. This is a way of saying that people will be able to move easily to see God. There will be nothing in the way when the whole world rushes joyfully to meet God, who gives us his loving presence.

Amazing things will happen. Weapons will be melted and reshaped into plows for farming. Instruments of hurt and death will be transformed into tools that help bring life and health. Where God rules, there will be no more enemies, only friends.

> Then the wolf shall be a guest of the lamb,
>   and the leopard shall lie down with the
>   young goat;
> The calf and the young lion shall browse
>   together,
>   with a little child to guide them. . . .
> They shall not harm or destroy on all my holy
>   mountain;
>   for the earth shall be filled with knowledge
>   of the Lord,
>   as water covers the sea. (Isaiah 11:6,9)

We read these hopeful and powerful words of Isaiah during Advent as we prepare for the coming of the Chosen One, Jesus. We prepare for him in three ways. First, by reading the Old Testament stories of God's people, we join them on their journey. When God's people of the old days are sad, we are sad. When they hope, we hope too. All together, we see how much the whole world needs God. With the people of the Old Testament stories, we wait patiently to see God fulfill the promise of a Chosen One.

Second, we pray about our journey right now. We admit that we have sinned, and that our sins keep us from walking close to God, going the right way. We pray more, and we listen closely so that we can prepare to meet Jesus now. We meet Jesus in the Sacrament of

Reconciliation so that we can experience the comfort God promises.

Third, we prepare for the future. The time of peace and harmony that God shows us in Isaiah's vision is not here yet, but it will be. Listening to Isaiah, we hear of God's power to bring all people together. We learn to see the world not with despair, but with hope!

If you want to read these prophecies from Isaiah in the Bible, go to Isaiah 40:1–11 and Isaiah 11:1–9.

Think Quietly: When do you need hope? What can you do to help people in your family hope and trust more in God?

Pray Together: Jesus, we have hope in you. Please come and reign in our hearts and in our home.

Prophets Describe the Messiah

God's people had all sorts of leaders in their history—men such as Abraham, Jacob, and Moses, judges such as Samson and Deborah, and prophets such as Isaiah and Samuel. The people of Israel were also led by kings.

The first three kings of Israel were Saul, David, and then David's son Solomon. David was considered the greatest of all the kings of Israel. So when the prophets said that one day all people would live in God's kingdom, the people thought the leader of this new kingdom would be like any other king. The prophets told them that God would raise up a great leader from the family of King David. Far in the future, God would rule through David's family. God would use a special son born in that family.

He it is who shall build a house for my name, and I will establish his royal throne forever. I will be a father to him, and he shall be a son to me. (2 Samuel 7:13–14)

Later, the prophet Isaiah said that God would give the people a sign that he was with them: a virgin would give birth to a son. This son would have a special name: *Emmanuel*, which means "God with us."

What kind of king would this Emmanuel be? Speaking through Isaiah the prophet, God told the people what their Messiah would be like:

> But a shoot shall sprout from the stump
> of Jesse,
> and from his roots a bud shall blossom.
> The spirit of the LORD shall rest upon him:
> a spirit of wisdom and of understanding,
> A spirit of counsel and of strength,
> a spirit of knowledge and of fear of the LORD.
> (Isaiah 11:1–2)

He would grow out of the "stump of Jesse"—this meant he would come from David's family. The Messiah would have the spirit of wisdom and understanding, of counsel, strength, knowledge, and fear of the Lord. Today, we call these qualities the Gifts of the Holy Spirit.

The Messiah would be fair. He would pay attention to the way people acted, not what they looked like. He would be a good shepherd, born in Bethlehem, and he would bring glad tidings to the poor. He would heal those with broken hearts, and he would set prisoners free.

Through a prophet named Zephaniah, God made the most amazing promise of all: God himself would be present in the Messiah. Through Emmanuel, God would dwell with the people.

> The LORD, your God, is in your midst,
> a mighty savior,
> Who will rejoice over you with gladness,
> and renew you in his love. (Zephaniah 3:17)

So, for hundreds of years, guided by the prophets, the people waited for this Messiah. They knew he would be fair and good and merciful. But when Jesus came, the people were confused. They were expecting a king who would be rich and powerful and live in a palace. Jesus was a descendant of King David, and he was born in Bethlehem, as the prophets had predicted. But Jesus was born in a stable, and his parents were just ordinary people—his father worked as a carpenter. Jesus lived with his parents and grew up in a poor, humble town, far away from Jerusalem, which was God's holy city. God's king would rule from Jerusalem—wouldn't he?

Jesus spoke with great wisdom, and he talked a lot about the Kingdom of God. But it was a strange kingdom, where a leader would have to serve others, and where people who were always first in line would be put at the back of the line. And in this kingdom, God's people would love their enemies. What about the Romans? The Roman Empire had treated God's people cruelly and ruled over them. Wouldn't the Messiah defeat the Roman soldiers and send them away? But Jesus never talked about that.

What sort of Messiah was this?

Jesus showed through his words and actions that he was fair and wise. And he had all the gifts of the Spirit, as the prophets had said he would. He healed people and freed them from the most powerful prisons of all: sin and death. He was the Messiah, and he lived among his people, not just like a human king, but as

God himself dwelling among us. His kingdom was different from what anyone expected, but it was real and would last forever.

❦

During Advent, we wait. We know Jesus, our Messiah and king, dwells among us, but we also know that we need to open our hearts to him and his kingdom. And we know that God has not finished doing his work in this world, so we wait to see what God will do today and tomorrow and the next day.

> Far in the future, God would rule through David's family.

We listen to the prophets' words about the Messiah because they remind us of who we are waiting for. When we make a Jesse Tree or sing "O Come, O Come, Emmanuel," we remember what God promised and how Jesus fulfills that promise.

We wait joyfully because the prophets have a message of hope for us. They tell us that no matter how confusing or painful life can be, we live in a kingdom guided by a Savior who loves us. In him, we find compassion, justice, peace, and freedom.

If you want to read these passages in the Bible, go to 2 Samuel 7:1–17; Isaiah 11:1–9; and Zephaniah 3:11–20.

Think Quietly: What did God tell his people their Messiah would be like?

Pray Together: Jesus, you are Lord and Messiah. In your kingdom, we find joy.

Zechariah Meets the Angel Gabriel

Near the city of Jerusalem lived a priest named Zechariah and his wife, Elizabeth. They were an elderly couple who had never had children. Zechariah served God as a priest.

In this time—not long before Jesus was born—the most important way a Jewish person could worship God was to offer sacrifice in the temple at Jerusalem. People gave the best of their animals and grain to the priests, who would sacrifice them to God in the innermost part of the temple, called the Holy of Holies. Priests also offered incense in the sanctuary of the temple. These sacrifices and prayers were spiritual routines for God's people—habits that helped them remember God's loving relationship with them.

One day, it was Zechariah's turn to go into the sanctuary and offer incense. Incense is made of plant materials, such as sap from a tree. When incense is burned, it makes a sweet smell, and it smokes. It was burned during worship so that the smoke drifting through the air would represent the people's prayers rising up to God. We still use incense in our worship today at the beginning of Mass, at the Gospel, at the Offertory, and at the elevation of the Host, and it represents our prayers going up to God, too.

Zechariah prayed in the holiest place of the temple. The people waited outside, praying. There were walls separating Zechariah from the people, but the prayers of the priest inside and the people outside joined to make one beautiful prayer to God.

Zechariah realized that an angel stood nearby.

The smoke and scent of incense filled the sanctuary while Zechariah prayed. But then, Zechariah realized that he was not alone.

An angel stood nearby. You can imagine how surprised and frightened Zechariah was. But the angel spoke to him:

"Do not be afraid, Zechariah, because your prayer has been heard. Your wife Elizabeth will bear you a son, and you shall name him John. And you will have joy and gladness, and many will rejoice at his birth, for he will be great in the sight of [the] Lord. . . . He will be filled with the holy Spirit even from his mother's womb, and he will turn many of the children of Israel to the Lord their God." (Luke 1:13–16)

Zechariah had a hard time understanding and believing what the angel was telling him. How could this be? he asked. He was old and so was Elizabeth. They were much too old to have a baby!

The angel told Zechariah that he was Gabriel, sent to bring Zechariah good news for his family and for all of Israel. But because Zechariah doubted, he would live with a sign of God's power: he would be mute, unable to speak, until God's promise was fulfilled.

Zechariah had been inside the temple sanctuary for a long time. The people praying outside started to wonder what was going on. When Zechariah came out, unable to speak, they knew that something unusual had happened.

Nine months passed. True to his promise, God gave Zechariah and Elizabeth a son. When it was time to name the boy, Zechariah was still mute, so it was Elizabeth who announced the baby's name: John. Her friends wondered why. Usually children were named after a family member, but no one in Zechariah's or Elizabeth's family was named John. The people were confused and went to Zechariah. Zechariah asked for a writing tablet and wrote his answer. He agreed with his wife: *His name is John*.

And at that moment, Zechariah could speak again! He was grateful that he could finally talk. But he was even more thankful that he had a new baby son. Full of joy, Zechariah prayed:

> And you, child, will be called prophet of the
> Most High,
>   for you will go before the Lord to prepare his
>   ways . . .
> to shine on those who sit in darkness and
>   death's shadow. (Luke 1:76,79)

A prayer like the one Zechariah said on that happy day is called a canticle, and the people of God pray the Canticle of Zechariah every day in the Church's Morning Prayer. It's a routine that keeps joy at the beginning of our day.

Our Advent and Christmas preparations are filled with traditions. We listen to the Scriptures read at church. We celebrate feasts of saints such as St. Nicholas and Our Lady of Guadalupe. We cook, we clean our homes, we clean our souls through confession, and we light candles.

Every day, we join our brothers and sisters around the world in preparing for the coming of the baby Jesus. When we pray Zechariah's joyful canticle, we join him in thanksgiving. We are grateful, we wait, and we trust as we follow our good habits of prayer and praise, knowing that any moment, God can burst through with a wonderful surprise!

If you want to read the whole story in the Bible, go to Luke 1:5–25 and 57–80.

Think Quietly: Can you remember a time when you were surprised by something wonderful happening? When do you know that God has blessed you?

Pray Together: Loving God, we trust in your promises to care for us and send us blessings.

The Annunciation

How do you know something important has happened? Is it because it happened to someone famous? Or it happened in a big city? Is an event important because we hear about it on television and the Internet? If everybody's talking about it, it must be important, right?

But think about this: the most important event in the history of the world happened in the life of someone who wasn't famous at all. And it happened in a place hardly anyone wanted to go.

It happened in the life of a girl named Mary.

Mary was just that—a girl. We don't know how old she was, but in this period of history, most young women married in their early teens. Mary was promised to be married to a man named Joseph; she was probably around fourteen years old.

Mary lived in Nazareth, a village in the northern part of the land we now call Israel, about seventy miles from Jerusalem. We don't know anything about Mary's life before we meet her in the Gospel of Luke. She wasn't a queen or a member of any powerful family. She was just a young woman who lived in a small town.

And then one day, an angel came to visit Mary. This angel was a messenger from God. His name was Gabriel, and he had surprising news for this young woman.

"Hail, full of grace, the Lord is with thee: blessed art thou among women."

Mary was confused. She wondered what this greeting was all about. The angel continued:

"Do not be afraid, Mary, for you have found favor with God. Behold, you will conceive in your womb and bear a son, and you shall name him Jesus. He will be great and will be called Son of the Most High, and the Lord God will give him the throne of David his father." (Luke 1:30–32)

During Advent, we listen to the words of the ancient prophets, so what the angel tells Mary sounds familiar to us. We have heard the prophets assure God's people that a time for rejoicing would come someday. We have heard them encourage the people to wait patiently because God would send them a Messiah from the house of David whose kingdom would bring peace and justice.

And right here in this quiet town, in the body of a young woman, that promise was about to be fulfilled.

There was a problem, though, and Mary pointed this out to the angel. She had never even been close to

> Mary wasn't a queen or a member of any powerful family.

a man, and she wasn't married. How could she have a baby?

The angel reminded Mary of God's great power. The book of Genesis tells us that when God began his mighty work of creation, the Spirit of God hovered over the water. God breathed life into the first man and woman. Now the angel told Mary, "The holy Spirit will come upon you, and the power of the Most High will overshadow you." (Luke 1:35) Her child, created by God in this way, would be called the Son of God.

Whenever we look at a baby, we see possibility. God helps us see his power to act in new ways when a baby is born. Young Mary, who was engaged but not married yet, and Joseph, her husband-to-be, would have a baby through the power of the Holy Spirit. This baby would be God's Son and the Savior of the world. This is why Gabriel told Mary to rejoice!

At that moment, in response to what the angel Gabriel had told her, Mary said yes to this news that would change her life and change the world. "Behold, I am the handmaid of the Lord. May it be done to me according to your word." (Luke 1:38)

Gabriel made two visits, to two people. First he went to Zechariah in the temple. Then he visited the home of Mary, a young woman who would not even be allowed to enter the place where Zechariah had offered incense.

～～

From the angel's words, we learn that Mary was very close to God. The angel greeted her as "full of grace." Every day at noon, around the world, people pray what we call the *Angelus*, repeating the greetings between Mary and Gabriel. And we remember how close Mary is to God every time we ask Mary to pray for us in the Hail, Mary prayer. We greet Mary the same way the angel did that day, and we ask for her prayers because she is so close to God. She is full of grace! We believe that, from the time Mary came to life in her mother's womb, God blessed her with grace and freedom from sin. This is the grace we celebrate on the feast of the Immaculate Conception.

God really is about to do something new. He is coming into the world, not in a temple with walls that only certain people can enter, but in a *person*. A humble, unknown person living in a small, unknown place.

When the angel Gabriel told Mary God's astonishing plan, God's people had been waiting many years for some good news. In this season of Advent, we are waiting too. And as we wait, we hear the same good news that Mary heard: God comes to save us and dwells in our midst, right here and now.

We wait, we pray, and we make ourselves ready for the most important moment of all. In Jesus, God comes to each of us. Like Mary, we can welcome him, put away fear, and say yes.

If you want to read the whole story in the Bible, go to Luke 1:26–38.

Think Quietly: How did Mary's yes change her life? When have you said yes to God?

Pray Together: Hail, Mary, the Lord is with thee!

Mary Visits Elizabeth

The angel Gabriel visited Mary, and her life changed. But Mary knew that this baby would not only change the lives of people in the family or their village. The angel told her that her baby was God's Promised One. This baby would grow up to change the world.

This was amazing news, and, of course, Mary wanted to share it. But who would believe her? Who would understand that her baby would be the Promised One? Well, Gabriel said that Mary's cousin Elizabeth was also going to have a special baby. Elizabeth's baby and Mary's baby would help God carry out the Good News for the world.

Elizabeth would understand what Mary was feeling. Elizabeth would help Mary think and pray about what God was doing in her life.

Cousin Elizabeth lived in another town, but Mary traveled as quickly as she could to go see her. She hurried to share her good news. She wanted to be close to someone who had been touched by God's grace in the same way she had. Probably Mary hoped she could help Elizabeth. After all, Elizabeth was an older woman who had never had a baby before. She could probably use some help!

Over the Judean hills Mary traveled, until she arrived at Zechariah and Elizabeth's house.

When Elizabeth heard Mary's greeting, the infant leaped in her womb, and Elizabeth, filled with the holy Spirit, cried out in a loud voice and said, "Most blessed are you among women, and blessed is the fruit of your womb." (Luke 1:41–42) She told Mary that when the child within her had heard her voice, he leaped for joy. Because of all the angel had revealed, Elizabeth knew that Mary's baby was chosen—so special that Elizabeth greeted Mary as "the mother of my Lord." (Luke 1:43)

Here in this house, two women greeted each other in joy. A baby in the womb recognized a holy presence and rejoiced. In these hidden places, far from worldly kings and powers, God was touching our human life and preparing a way for us to be close to him again.

Mary was filled with joy in this meeting with Elizabeth. They rejoiced together for the sons that would be born to both of them. Mary responded with this song:

> "My soul magnifies the Lord,
>   and my spirit rejoices in God my Savior,
> for he has looked with favor on the lowliness of
>   his servant.

> Elizabeth would understand what Mary was feeling.

Surely, from now on all generations will call
   me blessed. . . .
He has brought down the powerful from their
   thrones,
   and lifted up the lowly."

This is a prayer we still say and sing today. We call it the *Magnificat*, and Christians all over the world pray it every night as part of their evening prayer. When we pray this prayer, we are joining Mary in praising God. And when we welcome Mary into our hearts every night, we are welcoming Jesus, too, because Mary is the one who brings him to us, in joy.

Mary did stay and help Elizabeth, probably until the baby was born. Mary remained with her about three months and then returned to her home. (Luke 1:56)

During Advent, we prepare to meet Jesus. Mary shows us how. She shows us how one life can be part of God's great story. Every life—not just Mary's, but yours and mine—can help bring God's Good News to the world. Mary and Elizabeth show us how important it is to be generous to others, to share their joy. They show us how to welcome Jesus and to recognize his presence in all our friends and family, and especially in those who need our help. Like Mary, we can hurry to people who need us, bringing Jesus along, rejoicing on the journey!

If you want to read the whole story in the Bible, go to Luke 1:39–56.

Think Quietly: Why did Mary go to visit Elizabeth? Why did the baby John leap in Elizabeth's womb?

Pray Together: Blessed are you among women, and blessed is the fruit of your womb!

Joseph's Dream

Joseph lived a quiet life in a quiet town called Nazareth. He worked as a carpenter and was engaged to a young woman named Mary. The Scripture says they were *betrothed*. That means that they were engaged to be married. A betrothal was also a serious commitment between their two families. When two people became betrothed, their families announced this happy news to the whole town.

We meet Joseph in Matthew's Gospel, right after Matthew has shared a long list of Joseph's ancestors. This list reaches all the way back to Abraham, our father in the faith, whom God called to leave his home and travel to the Promised Land.

Abraham's son Isaac was on the list too, and so was Isaac's son Jacob. And, after several generations, we see another familiar name: David, the King of Israel. Joseph, the carpenter in Nazareth, was from King David's family. He was "of the house" of David. That doesn't mean that Joseph was a prince. It just means he was one of hundreds of descendants of King David's family. These descendants lived all over the Promised Land.

But the Promised Land was ruled by the Roman Empire. God's people, including Joseph, remembered that God had promised to send them a Messiah. The Messiah would save them and rule them with justice and peace. They knew that this Messiah would come from the house of David. But when? And who would be the Messiah?

Joseph lived an ordinary life—working, praying, and hoping for the Messiah. But then one day, Joseph heard some shocking news. Mary, the woman he was engaged to, was going to have a baby.

This was a big problem. Mary and Joseph were not yet married. Joseph was not the father of Mary's baby. He did not understand how Mary could be pregnant. It seemed that she had not kept her promise to love Joseph and no one else.

Joseph simply could not marry a woman who was going to have someone else's child. Everyone would understand if Joseph decided that Mary should stay with her own family.

Joseph was a kind man, and he did not want to embarrass Mary. He would not talk publicly about this situation. He would not announce that he had decided not to marry her after all. He would privately break their engagement and let Mary's family care for her and her child.

> This Messiah would come from the house of David. But when?

After making this decision, Joseph settled down to sleep. During the night, everything changed.

The angel Gabriel had told Zechariah that he would have a son. Gabriel had also announced to Mary that she would be the mother of Jesus. And now, in a dream, Joseph met an angel who brought him a message from God.

"Joseph, son of David, do not be afraid to take Mary your wife into your home. For it is through the holy Spirit that this child has been conceived in her. She will bear a son and you are to name him Jesus, because he will save his people from their sins."
(Matthew 1:20–21)

When the writer of Matthew's Gospel gathered Joseph's memories and passed them on to us, he remembered the words of the prophet Isaiah. Centuries before, Isaiah described a sign that God would give to show his power in this world: a young woman, a virgin, would have a baby.

> Behold, the virgin shall be with child and bear
> a son,
> and they shall name him Emmanuel.
> (Matthew 1:23)

Joseph had decided not to take Mary as his wife because he thought that was the best thing to do. But he didn't know everything, did he? When the angel appeared to him and told him who this baby was, Joseph understood much more. The baby would be the Messiah!

But the angel didn't say that Jesus would save the people from the Romans or from war or other trouble. He said that Jesus would save the people from their *sins*. How would he do that? Joseph knew that this baby would be the Messiah, but there was still a lot he didn't understand.

But, the angel told Joseph—and us—*don't be afraid!*

$$\smile$$

When God tells us, "Don't be afraid," he doesn't mean there won't be any problems or that we will understand everything. He means this: You're living your life in the way that is truthful and good. Trust the Lord who made and loves you.

During Advent, we remember other people like Joseph, who bravely accepted God's will. They're called saints. As we prepare for Christmas, we celebrate saints such as St. Francis Xavier, who traveled to distant lands with the Good News; St. Nicholas, who showed compassion for the poor; and St. Juan Diego, who bravely told the truth about seeing the Blessed Virgin, Our Lady of Guadalupe. All these people, along with Joseph, are on the journey with us as we try to follow the Lord's will and to live in goodness and hope.

On that journey, they're all with us. The angel's words are for us too. It's a time of hope.

Do not be afraid!

If you want to read the whole story in the Bible, go to Matthew chapter 1.

Think Quietly: How can Joseph's story help you overcome your fears?

Pray Together: St. Joseph, may your example help us bravely follow the Lord. St. Joseph, pray for us!

John the Baptist

There was a man named John who lived in Judea, near the Jordan River. His mother was Elizabeth, and his father was Zechariah. Do you remember Zechariah, who doubted the angel who told him his elderly wife would have a baby? Zechariah didn't believe the angel, so God took away Zechariah's voice.

But when the baby was born, Zechariah obeyed God and wrote on a tablet that the baby's name would be John. At that moment, Zechariah could speak again. That got people's attention! Something important was happening. This must be a special baby.

When John grew up, God led him into the desert, away from the crowds and noise of the towns. The desert was a lonely place, but it was quiet. Out there, John could listen to God.

And as John listened to God and learned what God was saying, John began to share it with others. He preached to whoever came to hear him. More and more people traveled out over the rocky land to see this man.

In those days John the Baptist appeared, preaching in the desert of Judea [and] saying, "Repent, for the kingdom of heaven is at hand!" . . . The whole region around the Jordan were going out to him and were being baptized by him in the Jordan River as they acknowledged their sins. (Matthew 3:1–2,5–6)

John didn't wear ordinary cloth robes. Instead, his clothes were made of rough camel's hair. He ate whatever the desert would give him: locusts, or grasshoppers, and honey that the bees made.

And by the waters of the river Jordan, John preached: "Repent! Repent!" He preached that God's kingdom was coming soon.

People who saw John and heard him preach thought he was strange. But he reminded them of the prophets from long ago—prophets such as Isaiah and Hosea. The people knew the stories about these prophets, about what they had said and some of the strange things they had done. They knew these stories by heart. When they went out to the desert and saw John, they thought he might be a prophet too. They remembered what Isaiah had said long ago:

> A voice of one crying out in the desert,
> "Prepare the way of the Lord,
>   make straight his paths." (Matthew 3:3)

When John cried out in the desert and urged the people to prepare, they remembered Isaiah, and they had hope. Was the Messiah coming?

The desert was a lonely place, but out there, John could listen to God.

Some people thought that maybe *John* was the Messiah. John said, "I am not the Messiah, but he's coming, and I'm helping you get ready to meet him."

John preached that people must turn from their sinful ways. When people decided to do this, John baptized them in the waters of the Jordan River. They wanted God to wash them clean from sin so they could start over and be closer to him. Being washed in the Jordan's waters was a sign of their new lives.

But getting baptized was only the beginning, John said. "I am baptizing you with water, for repentance, but the one who is coming after me is mightier than I. I am not worthy to carry his sandals. He will baptize you with the holy Spirit and fire." (Matthew 3:11)

John pointed the way. He was that voice the prophets had foretold, helping people prepare for the Messiah to come.

During Advent, we are busy with school projects and programs. We're busy getting ready for Christmas. Even though we are trying to celebrate Jesus' birth, we sometimes think more about all the work we're doing. We need to prepare for Christmas, but how? Should we buy more presents and cook more food? Should we decorate the house and get ready for holiday visitors? Probably we do those things.

But how do we prepare our *hearts* for Christmas? We can use Advent calendars and prayers. We can listen carefully to God's Word. Praying in a room with a flickering candle can give us the quiet we need to listen to God.

And maybe, this Advent, we can follow John the Baptist into the desert and listen to him. We can be honest about what's wrong in our lives, and we can repent. John lived out in a wild place, but it was quiet, too. During Advent, we need to make a quiet place in our hearts, so that God can speak to us. Then we can listen to God and prepare a place for Jesus in our lives.

Read more about John the Baptist in Mark 1:1–8; Matthew 3:1–11; Luke 3:2–18; and John 1:15–28.

Think Quietly: What was John the Baptist's message? How does this help us prepare the way for Jesus?

Pray Together: Lord, we are sorry for our sins. We want to clear the way in our hearts for you.

Christmas

Isaiah's Prophecies about the Messiah

Christmas and light just seem to go together. The lights of Christmas hang on the neighbors' houses, on stores, and in street decorations. Lights brighten the night. They surround us with color. Lights are everywhere, breaking through darkness.

At night in your house, maybe some Christmas lights are flickering. You might have lights on a Christmas tree or in an Advent wreath. Maybe candles line your windowsill or send a glow over your Nativity set. In a dark house, at the end of the day, candlelight can guide us from one room to another, helping us see.

In the middle of Christmas night, at midnight, churches around the world are filled with people of all ages. They gather, sing, and pray. They listen to God's Word. And the word on that night is about light!

> The people who walked in darkness
>   have seen a great light. (Isaiah 9:1)

No wonder we love to surround ourselves with lights at Christmas. We've seen a great light. His name is Jesus, and everywhere we go, we want to celebrate him!

Isaiah offered these words of hope to the people of Israel hundreds of years before Jesus was born. The people were going through hard times. They were afraid that Assyria, a huge empire near them, would attack them and take their land. The people of Israel thought that maybe they should make an agreement with Assyria. The Assyrians did not worship the God of Israel, but they could protect the people of Israel instead of attack them.

Isaiah listened to the people talk about how afraid they were. Isaiah also read God's Word. He prayed and opened his mind and heart to the Spirit of God so that he could lead the people to the truth and help them do what God wanted.

Isaiah spoke clearly and with great honesty. He told the people and the King of Israel that they just didn't trust God enough. They were moving away from God's strength and placing their hopes in false gods and the military power of the Assyrians. When we trust the world more than we trust God, we end up in darkness—terrible, sad darkness.

But in the Lord, there is light!

This is what God shows his people through Isaiah: God is more powerful than the darkness. His ways are light and peace.

And most exciting of all, God will send a leader from the family of King David to guide the people in this light and peace:

> For a child is born to us, a son is given us;
>   upon his shoulder dominion rests.
> They name him Wonder-Counselor, God-Hero,
>   Father-Forever, Prince of Peace. (Isaiah 9:5)

Isaiah's words gave comfort and joy to people hundreds of years before Jesus was born. When Jesus grew up and became a preacher and healer and teacher, people remembered what Isaiah had said about God's great leader. Then they saw what Jesus brought into the world through his life, death, and resurrection. They knew that Jesus was this promised child from the house of David who would reign in God's kingdom with justice and peace. They knew that Jesus was the Prince of Peace who was bringing comfort and joy that would never end.

We all walk in darkness sometimes, even now.

We are confused. We listen to voices in the world that tell us we are valuable only if we are important, talented, make good grades, or have certain clothes or things. We're like God's people when they thought God's strength wasn't enough. We need light!

We forget what good we can do in the world. We forget how much God loves every person we meet. We get stuck in sin and selfishness. We need light!

We're sad because we are sick, or people we love are sick. We're feeling lost because life has changed for us in some way. We are afraid of what might happen tomorrow. We need light!

Into this darkness, God comes. He comes as a baby who holds out his arms for our love.

The light has never stopped shining because Jesus' friends and followers have taught the truth, brought hope to the poor, prayed, created beauty, and loved as Jesus did.

The light flows from that manger in Bethlehem through the saints and all friends of Jesus over the centuries since his birth.

At Midnight Mass, we hear Isaiah tell us about that light. The light flickers from candles all around. The light burns steadily at the tabernacle, a sign that what the prophet foretold is true: the Prince of Peace has come and stays with us, a light shining in darkness, forever.

If you want to read the whole story in the Bible, go to Isaiah 9:1–6.

Think Quietly: What are your favorite kinds of light at Christmas? How is Jesus a light in your life? How is Jesus a light to the whole world?

Pray Together: Jesus, you are the light of our lives. Shine brightly in our darkness!

Into this darkness, God comes.

Two Mothers: Sarah and Hannah

In the story of God's people, God has shown his love through babies. Babies have always been a sign of hope and God's faithfulness.

Near the beginning of the history of his people, God called a man named Abraham to follow him, and Abraham did. He said yes to God. God led Abraham far from his home in the east to a new home in the land we now call Israel. Because God had promised this land to Abraham, it was called the Promised Land. There, God made a covenant with Abraham. A covenant is a special agreement or promise. Abraham agreed to be faithful to God. He promised to worship only the one true God. God agreed to protect Abraham and his family. God promised that Abraham's descendants would give light to the whole world by spreading the great news of God's love. To do that, Abraham had to have children and grandchildren, and God promised those, too—lots of them. Abraham would have many descendants, as many as the stars in the sky and the sand on the seashore.

What an awesome promise! This covenant between God and Abraham would last through all the generations.

But there was a problem. Abraham didn't have any children. Not even one son or daughter. And Abraham and his wife, Sarah, were already old. In fact, Sarah's body was too old to become pregnant and give birth. God's promise was wonderful, but wasn't it too late? How could two old people have descendants as numerous as the stars?

One day, Abraham was sitting outside his tent, staying cool under the trees during the hottest part of the day. He saw some strangers approaching.

In Abraham's time, it was important to help people who were traveling, even if they were strangers. If a traveler was not invited into people's homes, he might not find food or water or a place to sleep. Abraham jumped up when he saw the strangers. Right away he offered them something to drink and eat. And he told them to rest there in the shade.

While they ate, the visitors talked with Abraham.

"Where is your wife Sarah?" they asked him. "There in the tent," he replied. One of them said, "I will return to you about this time next year, and Sarah will then have a son." Sarah was listening at the entrance of the tent, just behind him. (Genesis 18:9–10)

When Sarah heard the visitor say that she and Abraham would have a baby next year, she laughed out loud. She was too old! What a ridiculous thing for this stranger to say!

> God's promise was wonderful, but wasn't it too late?

But this was no ordinary stranger; it was a messenger from God. Sarah did get pregnant. And one year later, she gave birth to a boy. They named him Isaac. Guess what that name means? "He laughs."

Little Isaac grew up and had children. And his children had children, and *their* children had children. And on and on. So Abraham did have many descendants: the Jewish people. Through them, the light and wisdom of God's law spread through the whole world.

Centuries after Abraham and Sarah, another woman wanted with all her heart to have a baby. Her name was Hannah, and she was not old like Sarah, but she could not get pregnant. She and her husband had hoped for years to have a child, but none came.

Hannah prayed for a child, and she made a promise to God. If God gave her a son, she would give that son right back to God. Her son would serve God in the temple.

One day, Hannah was at the temple, praying for God to give her a baby. This was such an emotional prayer that she spoke it out loud and wept. Eli the priest thought she was drunk, and he scolded her.

Hannah told the priest that she was not drunk—just very sad because she couldn't have a child. She prayed from the deepest place in her heart.

Eli listened. He told her to go in peace, and he prayed with her that God would answer her prayer.

Before very long, Hannah's prayer was answered. She had a son! She named him Samuel, which means "God has heard."

When Samuel was old enough, Hannah kept her promise to God, because God had been faithful to her and given her a child. Hannah took little Samuel back to Eli at the temple, where he would grow up and learn about God's Word.

Hannah could have been sad, but she was joyful. She knew that her baby was God's gift to her. This little son was not her possession. The baby had been created by God and was on earth to play a part in God's plan. This filled Hannah with joy, and so she prayed and sang a canticle:

> My heart exults in the LORD,
>   my [strength] is exalted by my God. . . .

> He raises the needy from the dust;
>   from the ash heap [he] lifts up the poor.
>   (1 Samuel 2:1,8)

Do Hannah's words sound familiar? Hundreds of years later, another woman prayed and sang when *she* was having a child in a miraculous way. It was Mary, whose canticle we call the *Magnificat*. She sang it when she was pregnant with Jesus and visited Elizabeth, who was pregnant with John.

Hannah and Mary both sang about the greatness of God who had given them—and the world—these children. As mothers, they were blessed with children. But as women who trusted in God, they understood that their sons were not for them alone. God would work through the life of Hannah's son to help the people of Israel. And through Mary's son, Jesus, God would bless the whole world.

Read more about Sarah and Hannah in Genesis 18:1–15; Genesis 21:1–7; and 1 Samuel 1—2:10.

Think Quietly: How were the babies Isaac, Samuel, and Jesus all signs of God's power and love?

Pray Together: Loving Father, thank you for the gift of life. Thank you for the gift of your Son, Jesus.

Jesus Is Born

The people of Israel had been waiting for a Savior and a king, and there he was, quietly hidden. Only his parents, some animals, and a few shepherds were there to see him.

It happened in Bethlehem, a town just a few miles from Jerusalem.

Mary and Joseph didn't live in Bethlehem. Their home was in Nazareth, far to the north. But they had to travel to Bethlehem because the Roman government ordered all the people to pay a new tax. To do this, they had to travel back to the town their family came from. Joseph was from the family—the "house"—of David, and the family home was Bethlehem. So Joseph and his wife, Mary, traveled there.

What a difficult journey it was. It was almost time for Mary to have her baby, so she was probably tired much of the time. And because everyone else was traveling to pay their taxes, the road was crowded and noisy. We know that Bethlehem was busy and crowded. Luke's Gospel tells us:

While they were there, the time came for her to have her child, and she gave birth to her firstborn son. She wrapped him in swaddling clothes and laid him in a manger, because there was no room for them in the inn. (Luke 2:6–7)

A manger was a feeding trough for animals. Mary had her baby out where the cows and sheep were staying! In Hebrew, *Bethlehem* means "house of bread." Who could know that this baby would grow up to be the Savior of the world, and he would call himself the "Bread of Life"? For now, Jesus lay there in a manger, which held food for the animals to eat. With only animals to see, God came to earth as a baby.

It is a scene we know well. We've seen paintings of it and movies about it. We have also seen Nativity sets in our own homes and churches. Maybe we've even acted out the Nativity story. More than a thousand years after the birth of Jesus, St. Francis of Assisi thought that seeing the scene of Jesus' birth would help us grow closer to God. In a small Italian town, St. Francis gathered women, men, children, and animals to create the very first Nativity scene.

Outside Bethlehem, not far from where Jesus lay, shepherds were watching their flocks of sheep. The lives of shepherds were hard. They had to watch their fields day and night and protect their sheep from thieves and predators.

Shepherds were some of the poorest people in Jewish society. They often were outcasts, too. They had to care for animals every day, which meant that they disobeyed religious law by working on the Sabbath.

They often had to touch animals that had diseases, and they got bloody sometimes when an animal was injured. Religious law said that a person who touched blood or disease was unclean and could not be close to God or come close to where people worshipped God. So shepherds were outsiders, and people looked down on them.

But the shepherds weren't outcasts to God or the angels.

Now there were shepherds in that region living in the fields and keeping the night watch over their flock. The angel of the Lord appeared to them and the glory of the Lord shone around them, and they were struck with great fear. The angel said to them, "Do not be afraid; for behold, I proclaim to you good news of great joy that will be for all the people. For today in the city of David a savior has been born for you who is Messiah and Lord." (Luke 2:8–11)

Once again, the angels told people not to be afraid, because there was good news! The Messiah was born! The angels even told the shepherds how to find him:

And this will be a sign for you: you will find an infant wrapped in swaddling clothes and lying in a manger. (Luke 2:12)

How strange! The people were waiting for the Messiah, but in their minds, he would be powerful, and everyone would know it was him. But could the Messiah be this newborn baby, wrapped in cloth and lying in a feed trough?

Jesus' humble birth showed us that God does things in ways we don't expect.

> Glory to God in the highest
>   and on earth peace to those on whom his
>   favor rests. (Luke 2:14)

This is what the angels sang after they shared the good news. It is such good news that we sing it almost every

Sunday in Mass, giving glory to God for coming among us and joining heaven to earth!

After the angels left, the shepherds hurried to see Jesus. They told Mary and Joseph what the angels had said. Mary treasured all they had told her. She kept these amazing memories in her heart to think and pray about always.

The shepherds were watching and waiting for signs. When the good news came, they did not waste a moment. They rushed to see Jesus. They hurried as fast as they could. Will we follow the shepherds' example?

God has made himself small for us. God waits for us. The baby is born! Let us hurry to see him and give glory to God for his love!

Christmas has begun!

Could the Messiah be this baby, wrapped in cloth and lying in a feed trough?

To read the whole story in the Bible, go to Luke 2:1–20.

Think Quietly: Think about what a baby is like. Think about what it means that God came to us, born as a baby. Why is this good news?

Pray Together: Glory to God in the highest! And peace to all people on earth!

The Magi Bring Their Gifts

When we look up into a night sky, what do we see?

Lights flicker and glow and move across the heavens. We watch the stars, and some people study them, to learn about this great universe God has created. The night sky has always made people wonder. Where did they come from? Who made them? Where do we fit in with the stars, earth, and the whole universe?

When Jesus was born in Bethlehem of Judea, in the days of King Herod, behold, magi from the east arrived in Jerusalem, saying, "Where is the newborn king of the Jews? We saw his star at its rising and have come to do him homage." (Matthew 2:1–2)

Long ago, some wise men studied the stars. They lived far from Bethlehem, perhaps in the lands of Persia or Arabia. These men, called *magi*, had noticed a certain star. Their studies showed that this star was a sign of something new and wonderful: a new king of the Jews was about to be born. These wise men decided to follow the star and find this king. Their travels brought them to the land of Israel, among the Jewish people.

When King Herod heard this, he was greatly troubled, and all Jerusalem with him. (Matthew 2:3)

At this time, the land of Israel, along with most other areas around the Mediterranean Sea, was part of the Roman Empire, which was huge and powerful. The Romans allowed the people they ruled to have some freedom. God's people had to obey the Roman emperor. But the emperor chose a man named Herod to serve as the Jewish king. Herod ruled his people, but he also had to do whatever the Romans told him to do.

Herod heard about the magi—these men from the east—and the questions they were asking. He gathered his advisors and asked them to think about what the magi had said. Was there really a new king of the Jews? And if so, where could they find him?

> These men, called *magi*, had noticed a certain star.

The Jewish scribes and teachers thought about the prophets and the history of God's people. They reflected on words from the prophet Micah.

They said to [Herod], "In Bethlehem of Judea, for thus it has been written through the prophet:

And you, Bethlehem, land of Judah,
 are by no means least among the rulers
  of Judah;
since from you shall come a ruler,
 who is to shepherd my people Israel."
 (Matthew 2:5–6)

The new king would come from nearby Bethlehem!

This upset Herod because he didn't want a new king to take his place. But he was careful not to show this. He told the magi to go to Bethlehem and find the new king. Then, they should come back and tell him all about it. Of course, he would want to worship this king, too!

The wise men left Herod, left Jerusalem, and continued their journey. They kept following the star, and finally it stopped. It stopped over the place where Mary, Joseph, and Jesus were.

Then they opened their treasures and offered him gifts of gold, frankincense, and myrrh. (Matthew 2:11)

The magi had brought gifts. They were gifts for a king, and they remind us of Jesus in different ways. The gold reminds us that Jesus really is king, the ruler of the stars and all creation, and Lord of our lives. The frankincense reminds us that Jesus is a priest who reaches between heaven and earth, the one who shows us the face of God. Myrrh was used by the people of Jesus' time to anoint the bodies of those who had died, so this gift of myrrh reminds us that Jesus would rule over everything, even death.

The magi were delighted to see this new king. After they offered their gifts, they returned to their home country. Because they were warned in a dream, they did not trust King Herod to be kind to the baby king. They did not return to see him or tell him anything about Jesus.

The magi were right about Herod. The king was afraid for any other king to be in Israel. He wanted this power for himself. But he didn't know how to find the baby Jesus. So he sent soldiers to kill all boys under the age of two. That way, he would be sure to get rid of the new king.

But God warned Joseph in a dream that Herod planned to kill Jesus. So Joseph took Mary and the baby away to Egypt, and they lived there until Herod died and it was safe for them to return home.

God was drawing people to see Jesus. The first visitors were the poor and outcast shepherds. And then, God worked through creation to spread the news even further. A light from heaven called people from outside Israel to see God's love in the form of a baby. God's love and light invite everyone to journey to see his face.

⁓

When the magi gave their gifts to Jesus, they inspired us to be generous, too. In many parts of the world, gifts are exchanged twelve days after Christmas Day. This gift day is called the Feast of the Epiphany, Three Kings' Day, or Día de los Reyes.

The magi also knew that God teaches us who he is through his creation. They knew that signs of God's presence are everywhere. They were humble, brave, and determined enough to set out on a long, hard journey because of the new star and its message.

And then, when they saw Jesus, they knew that life would be different forever. They had seen God's beauty, truth, and love. The magi went back changed—different from how they were before they saw Jesus. Matthew's Gospel tells us that "they departed for their country by another way."

It's the way of Jesus, and once we meet him, it's our way, too.

If you want to read the whole story in the Bible, go to Matthew chapter 2.

Think Quietly: What does nature tell us about God? What does the baby Jesus tell us about God?

Pray Together: Jesus, you are wisdom. Enlighten our hearts and our minds.

Jesus Is the Word of God

At Christmastime, when we go to church and read the Bible in our homes, we most often listen to the stories of Jesus' birth in Matthew and Luke. But when we go to Mass on Christmas morning, we hear something different. We hear the beginning of the first chapter of the Gospel of John.

> In the beginning was the Word,
>   and the Word was with God,
>   and the Word was God. (John 1:1)

John's Gospel doesn't begin by telling us the history of Jesus' family background. John's Gospel doesn't even talk about Jesus being born or about any of his early life. John goes all the way back to the beginning of the world—"In the beginning . . ." Does that remind you of anything?

In the beginning, when God created the heavens and the earth . . . God said, "Let there be light," and there was light. (Genesis 1:1,3)

When John says, "In the beginning was the Word," he is telling us that Jesus was there in the very beginning of creation.

> All things came to be through him,
>   and without him nothing came to be.
> What came to be through him was life,
>   and this life was the light of the human race;
> the light shines in the darkness,
>   and the darkness has not overcome it.
>   (John 1:3–5)

Through these mysterious words, John describes Jesus.

God is a mystery, which means that God is beyond human understanding. We can know a little about God through the beauty and order of creation. We can know about God because we are made in God's image, with the ability to think and create and love. But God wants us to know him and love him. So God *reveals* himself to us. He tells us about himself.

God revealed himself to Abraham and Sarah and many others in the history of God's people. He revealed himself through prophets such as Isaiah. But still, that wasn't enough.

> And the Word became flesh
>   and made his dwelling among us,
>   and we saw his glory,
>   the glory as of the Father's only Son,
>   full of grace and truth. (John 1:14)

God revealed himself by coming to earth. We don't have to wonder who God is anymore. We don't have to wonder what God is like, because Jesus has revealed what God is like. "The Word was with God, and the Word was God." That's why we say in the Creed, "God from God, light from light, true God from true God."

You might remember that in Genesis, every time God created, he spoke. "God said, 'Let there be light.'" With words, God created us. John calls Jesus the Word, because the whole universe came to exist through Jesus.

When John said, "The Word became flesh and made his dwelling among us," he was saying that the Word "pitched his tent among us." That's what it means in the Greek language, which is what John used when he wrote the Gospel.

In the centuries before Jesus, when God's people wandered in the desert, they kept the Ark of the Covenant with them always. Inside the Ark was the written-down law that God had given to Moses. Before God's people ever had a temple, they had a tent where they kept the Ark of the Covenant. This was called the Tent of Meeting. The people believed that God was present there. You could say that God had "pitched a tent" to stay among them.

But only a few people God chose could ever go into the Tent of Meeting or be near the Ark of the Covenant. God's presence dwelled with the people, but they could not truly be close to God.

Then, when Jesus came, he lived among us, and people could come up to him. They could talk to him, hug him, laugh or cry with him. "The Word became flesh" means that Jesus became one of us. And during his life on earth, he lived among poor people, ordinary people. God's great light of love shone out of the person, Jesus of Nazareth. Jesus was the perfect Word who could speak to us clearly about God.

Sometimes it's hard to say exactly what you mean, isn't it? It's so frustrating when we can't find the words to tell how we feel! Words don't always work as well as we want them to. But God's Word, Jesus, became a person who could tell us through his words—but also through his actions—everything we need to know about who God is and how much God loves us.

Read all about how John described Jesus in John 1:1–18.

Think Quietly: What are some words that describe Jesus? Jesus is the Word of God. What does he tell us about God?

Pray Together: Jesus, Word of God, we are listening to you.

And the Word became flesh and made his dwelling among us.

Ordinary Time

Isaac and His Sons, Jacob and Esau

In the Bible, we find the family stories of God's people. And all kinds of stories are included. When God's people passed down the stories of their family history, they didn't pretend that every person had always made good decisions. They trusted that the Lord could bring good out of anything, even our sins.

After our first parents and the Flood, the world continued its bumpy course. Human beings had misused the gift of free will and distorted the beauty of God's creation, but God never stopped reaching out to them. He had made a covenant with Abraham, promising that his family would be a light to the nations.

Abraham's son Isaac married, and after years and many prayers, his wife Rebekah became pregnant—with twins! This was a strange, difficult time for Rebekah. It felt as if the two babies were always fighting inside her. When the babies were born, the one they named Esau came out first, and then his twin brother came, and they named him Jacob.

Because Esau was a few minutes older, he had the family birthright. The birthright went to the oldest son in the family. This meant that when Isaac died, Esau would be the head of the household and would receive a much larger inheritance than any of the other sons. The birthright was very important in a family. It was a privilege but also a big responsibility.

Esau grew up to be a hunter, and most of the time he wandered in the countryside outside the family camp. Remember that Isaac's people were nomads, who lived in tents and traveled with their goats and sheep from place to place. Jacob preferred to work inside the camp, caring for the tents and supplies and doing other jobs closer to home.

One day, Jacob was in the camp, cooking a lentil stew. Esau, who had been out in the field for a long time, returned, and he was hungry. He asked Jacob for some of the stew. Jacob agreed, but Esau would have to pay a price. "First sell me your right as firstborn," (Genesis 25:31) Jacob said.

Have you ever done something and then later realized that you should have thought about what the consequences would be? Or have you been tempted to do something that seemed small—cheat a little or say something that wasn't a big lie but wasn't really the truth? Then you learned that this small thing had bigger consequences than you expected.

Esau was hungry. And he would not receive his birthright until their father was dead—that could be years from now! What use was his birthright today? He agreed to trade his birthright for a bowl of stew. This was a secret between Jacob and Esau for many years.

The day did come when their father, Isaac, was dying. It was time for him to give the birthright blessing, to pass to his oldest son responsibility for the family and most of the family property. Isaac was nearly blind. He called Esau and told him to go hunting and then prepare him his favorite food. It would be a feast, and Isaac would give Esau his blessing. Then everyone would know that Esau now had his birthright and would become head of the household.

Rebekah overheard this conversation. Her favorite son was Jacob, so she told him to go get two of the best baby goats, and she would prepare them just the way Isaac liked them. Then Jacob would go to his father, pretending to be Esau. He would give his father the meal, and Isaac would give Jacob the birthright blessing.

Jacob saw a problem, though. His father would know that he wasn't Esau because Esau was hairy and Jacob had smooth skin. If Isaac touched Jacob, he would know that Jacob and his mother had tried to trick him. Then Isaac would not give Jacob a blessing, but a curse! Rebekah gave him Esau's clothes to wear and covered Jacob's arms and neck with the skin from the slaughtered baby goats.

The trick worked. Isaac thought Jacob was his son Esau. And so Isaac blessed him:

> May peoples serve you,
>   and nations bow down to you;
> Be master of your brothers,
>   and may your mother's sons bow down to
>   you. (Genesis 27:29)

Not long after that, Esau came to his father, and they figured out what Rebekah and Jacob had done—they had tricked Isaac into giving his birthright blessing to the wrong son! Esau begged his father to give him the blessing, but the blessing could not be undone. And remember, Esau had traded away his birthright years before. But he blamed his brother, Jacob, and became furious with him.

For his own safety from Esau's anger, Jacob returned to the home of his mother's family, far away in Haran. On the way there, he had a strange dream: a ladder stood between heaven and earth, and angels were climbing up and down on it. As Jacob dreamed, God came to him and shared the same promises he had shared with Abraham and Isaac: a promise of God's presence, protection, and love. Jacob woke from the dream and named this special place where he had met God. He called the place Bethel.

Many years later, Jacob returned to his homeland. He had become a wealthy man, and he brought with him a large family of wives, children, and servants. They brought with them all their sheep, goats, camels, cows, and donkeys. Jacob was afraid that, even after all this time, his brother, Esau, would attack and kill him.

So the night before he was to approach his brother, Jacob sent all his family and their animals away. He laid down to rest, and while he rested, someone came to him, and in the dark of night, he challenged Jacob and they wrestled.

They fought until daybreak. Jacob was staying strong, and when his opponent saw that he could not win, he struck Jacob in the hip and told Jacob to let him go. Jacob said he would not until his opponent blessed him. What was his name? the man asked. Jacob told him.

Esau traded his birthright for a bowl of stew.

"You shall no longer be named Jacob, but Israel, because you have contended with divine and human beings and have prevailed." (Genesis 32:29) The name God gave him—*Israel*—means "God will prevail."

In the mystery of strange encounters and dreams, through human weakness and sin, God does prevail. When Jacob met Esau the next day, Esau ran to meet him, embraced him, and flinging himself on his neck, kissed him as he wept. (Genesis 33:4) God uses all that happens to us—the good and the bad—to reach down and draw us closer to him.

To read the whole story in the Bible, go to Genesis 27—33:4.

Think Quietly: Why did Esau give up his birthright? What did Jacob's encounters with God reveal to him? How can we sometimes be like Esau and trade our "birthright" for something less important?

Pray Together: Lord, you have given me life and blessing. Help me always value your love above everything else.

Joseph's Troubles and God's Plan

Jacob had many, many sons. Twelve, in fact.

Sometimes in a family, we wonder if parents favor one child over the others, and this seemed true in Jacob's family. The problem was that Jacob, who had two wives, loved one—Rachel—more than the other, Leah. And he loved Rachel's sons, Joseph and Benjamin, more than he loved Leah's sons. Over the years, the older brothers grew tired of this. They could see that their father loved Joseph more than any of them. Jacob even gave Joseph a beautiful coat.

Even worse, Joseph started talking about his dreams. And in those dreams, Joseph was important, and his brothers had to honor him. The older brothers had had enough. They sold Joseph to some traders who were passing through their land. Then Joseph's brothers sprinkled goat's blood on his beautiful coat and told their father that some animal must have killed Joseph.

The traders sold Joseph to an Egyptian court official named Potiphar. But the LORD was with Joseph and he enjoyed great success and was assigned to the household of his Egyptian master. When his master saw that the LORD was with him and brought him success in whatever he did, he favored Joseph and made him his personal attendant; he put him in charge of his household and entrusted to him all his possessions. (Genesis 39:2–4)

It didn't take long, though, for Joseph to run into trouble again. This time, Potiphar's wife made a false accusation against him, and Joseph was put in prison. Surely this was the end for him.

But then, Pharaoh's cupbearer and his baker, who were in prison with Joseph, had strange dreams. Joseph had a gift for interpreting dreams, so he offered to interpret theirs. Joseph had good news and bad news. The cupbearer's dream meant that he would be freed from prison and work for the Pharaoh again. But the baker? His dream of birds pecking at his head meant that he would be beheaded.

> They sold Joseph to some traders who were passing through their land.

Both dreams came true, but the servant who got his job back didn't remember to mention Joseph and his gift to the Pharaoh. So Joseph spent two more years in prison.

Then Pharaoh started having disturbing dreams. His servant remembered that Joseph could interpret dreams, and he told the Pharaoh about this. Joseph was brought out of prison to listen to the Pharaoh describe his dreams. In the first dream, seven sickly cows ate up seven fat and healthy cows. In the second dream, seven thin ears of corn swallowed up seven fat ears.

Joseph knew the meaning of these dreams right away, and he explained them to the Pharaoh. Egypt would enjoy seven years of prosperity and good crops. But these seven years of plenty would be followed by seven years when the crops failed and there would be no food for the people. Joseph told the Pharaoh that it was important to manage the country's resources. During the seven prosperous years, they needed to store the extra food for the seven years when the crops would fail.

The Pharaoh was so impressed by Joseph that he put Joseph in charge of Egypt's food. When the seven good years came, Joseph made certain that the country stored the extra for the hard years. Then the hard years came—the years of famine, when there was not enough food from the crops and the livestock. But Joseph's plan had worked, and there was enough food stored up for everyone.

There was famine in the Promised Land of Canaan, too, where Joseph's family still lived. Jacob heard that there was food in Egypt, so he sent all his sons there to get food for them. But he did not send his youngest son, Benjamin, who was Joseph's younger brother.

When the sons of Jacob arrived in Egypt, Joseph recognized them, but they did not recognize him. Joseph noticed that his younger brother, Benjamin, was not with them. Joseph longed to see his younger brother after so many years! So he accused the brothers of being spies. They protested and told him they only came to buy food for their starving families. They described their large family to him, including their youngest brother, Benjamin, who had stayed at home.

Joseph made a deal with them. He would sell them the grain, but to prove they were not spies, they must leave one brother in Egypt as a prisoner. Then they would return home and bring to him this younger brother they had spoken of, to prove that their story was true. Only when Joseph saw Benjamin would he free the brother who was in prison.

Reuben, the oldest, spoke to his brothers in their own language. He said that this seemed unfair, but it was what they deserved for selling Joseph years ago and causing such grief for their father, Jacob. Joseph understood every word. He heard Reuben admit his guilt. After all these years, Joseph knew that his brothers were sorry for how they had treated him. Joseph had to leave them for a few moments to cry in private.

Simeon agreed to stay in Egypt until the rest returned. They did, this time with Benjamin. They purchased grain, Simeon was released, and Joseph saw his younger brother. But still, Joseph did not tell them that he was their brother. He still wasn't sure that his brothers had changed. He arranged another test for them. He gave his own silver cup to a servant and told the servant to hide the cup in one of Benjamin's sacks of food.

After they had gone a little way toward home, the brothers were stopped by Egyptian officials. Someone, they said, had stolen Joseph's silver cup. The brothers denied it, and they said that if they found the cup in any of their sacks, that person who owned the sack would die. The sacks were searched. They sifted through grain, and in Benjamin's sack they found the silver cup.

Brokenhearted, the brothers returned to Joseph. Benjamin would not be killed, he said, but would remain in Egypt as his slave. The rest could go. Judah stepped forward. He told Joseph their family story, and how important Benjamin was to Jacob. If they returned to Canaan without him, Jacob would surely die. And so, Judah said, he would take his place. He could not bear to see his father suffer so.

Judah's offer to take his little brother's place showed Joseph that his brothers had learned compassion.

"I am your brother Joseph," he said to them, "whom you sold into Egypt." (Genesis 45:4)

The brothers were astonished and overjoyed. But they were also afraid. What would Joseph do to them? Here is what Joseph said to them:

"But now do not be distressed, and do not be angry with yourselves for having sold me here. It was really for the sake of saving lives that God sent me here ahead of you. . . . So it was not really you but God who had me come here; and he has made me a father to Pharaoh." (Genesis 45:5,8)

We know this from our lives, don't we? Good changes have come out of moments that we thought at the time were nothing but bad. And they probably *were* bad. But God can use them to help us come closer to him if we have an open heart and if we trust God to care for us.

To read the whole story in the Bible, go to Genesis chapters 37—50.

Think Quietly: What good did God bring out of Joseph's suffering? What good does God bring out of Jesus' suffering?

Pray Together: Lord of all, you are more powerful than any darkness. Help us find ways to bring good out of hard times.

God Calls Moses

After Joseph forgave his brothers, they moved their whole family to Egypt. Then, many generations passed, and the number of Israelites in Egypt grew into a huge population.

The present Pharaoh and other Egyptian leaders had forgotten all about Joseph, the Israelite who was a good leader for them, who had saved the whole country from starving. That happened a long time ago. Now the Pharaoh was worried that all the Israelites would become too powerful and take over his country. So he took away their rights as citizens and turned them into slaves. He put the Israelites to work, and they were forced to do the hardest jobs in the kingdom. They were treated badly and suffered for many years.

The Pharaoh had another plan to keep the Israelite population from growing: all their baby boys should be killed by the midwives who delivered them. Midwives were like nurses, and they helped women when they were having their babies. Midwives felt that it was their responsibility to bring life into the world and help all babies survive and live. They refused to kill the babies they helped deliver. Then the Pharaoh said that any baby boy born to the people of Israel must be thrown into the Nile River.

One Israelite woman did not throw her baby boy into the river. She hid him as long as she could. But when he grew too big to hide from the Egyptians, she placed him in a basket and sent him floating down the Nile River. She sent the baby's big sister to follow the basket and see what would happen.

Along came the Pharaoh's own grown daughter, coming to the river to bathe. She saw the child and could tell that it was an Israelite baby who should have been thrown into the river. But she felt compassion for the little boy and decided to adopt him. The baby's sister came up to the Pharaoh's daughter and offered to find a nurse for the baby. The Pharaoh's daughter agreed, so the girl went and got her mother. And so the baby's mother was able to take care of him while he grew up in the Pharaoh's palace.

Pharaoh's daughter named the boy Moses, which means "drawn out of the water."

Moses' life had a special beginning, and he was lucky to be brought up as the adopted son of the Pharaoh's daughter. But he knew he was an Israelite, and one day he saw an Egyptian beating an Israelite slave. In his anger, Moses killed the Egyptian. When he learned that others had seen this, he knew that he must leave Egypt.

Moses went away from Egypt and to the land of Midian. There, he joined a nomadic tribe. Moses married one of the women, and they had a son. Moses had escaped trouble in Egypt. Now he spent his days tending sheep. Probably he thought he would stay here in Midian for the rest of his life, working with his family.

But back in Egypt, life was getting worse for God's people. The Pharaoh worked them harder and harder. They suffered, and they prayed to God for freedom.

Out in the wilderness of Midian, Moses was tending the flocks of his father-in-law. He took them all over the land, and ended up at a mountain called Horeb. There in the wild lands, surrounded by sheep, Moses saw something very strange. A bush seemed to be on fire. But when Moses looked more closely, he could see that the bush was on fire but it was not being burnt up. God called out to him from the bush: Moses! Moses! He answered, "Here I am." God said: Do not come near! Remove the sandals from your feet, for the place where you stand is holy ground. I am the God of your father, he continued, the God of Abraham, the God of Isaac, and the God of Jacob. (Exodus 3:4–6)

God told Moses that he had heard the cries of his people. He had seen their sufferings, and now God would free them. He would take them back to the Promised Land, the land he had promised Abraham, the land flowing with milk and honey.

And Moses was the one who would lead them there. Moses would go to Pharaoh and tell him it was God's will that the people of Israel be freed and allowed to return to their home.

Moses knew that this would be hard to explain to the people back in Egypt. Why should they believe him? How would they know he was telling the truth and that God really had called him to lead them?

This is how: God would tell him his name. God replied to Moses: I am who I am. Then he added: This is what you will tell the Israelites: I AM has sent me to you.

God spoke further to Moses: "This is what you will say to the Israelites: The LORD, the God of your ancestors, the God of Abraham, the God of Isaac, and the God of Jacob, has sent me to you." (Exodus 3:14–15)

Moses, a descendant of Abraham, would carry this good news to the people of Israel: their God, the only God, was real, was powerful, and would save them. His power and love would be not just for them, but for the whole world to see. It would be a light to the nations.

God does not depend on anything or anyone else. God just *is*. That's what the name he revealed to Moses means. It is a holy name, which the Jewish people, even today, do not pronounce out loud. It means, in English, *I AM*.

> Back in Egypt, life was getting worse for God's people.

Once Jesus was having a discussion with Pharisees. It was after he had met the woman about to be stoned for her sin, and he had told her that her sins were forgiven.

The Pharisees gathered around and said to Jesus, "Only God can forgive sins!" They were saying to Jesus, "Who do you think you are?"

And here is Jesus' answer: "Amen, amen, I say to you, before Abraham came to be, I AM." (John 8:58)

To read the whole story in the Bible, go to Exodus chapters 1—4.

Think Quietly: Why was Moses surprised that God would choose him to be a leader of the Israelites?

Pray Together: Loving God, you used Moses to lead your people to freedom. May we always be ready to serve you and do your will.

Joshua Leads God's People

The time had come. The Promised Land lay just across the Jordan River.

After years of journeying in the wilderness, the people of God were almost back home, to the land God had promised their fathers long ago. They had suffered much, and they had complained. But God had led them every step of the way. The people grew closer as a community by learning and obeying the Law, which was the way of life God had explained to them through Moses on Mount Sinai. God called the Israelites to be a light to the world. They answered yes to that call, and now it was time to take the next step.

But Moses would not be with them. As they looked down upon the land, Moses reminded the people of all that God had done for them. He reminded them that they lived in a sacred agreement—a covenant—with God "so that he may establish you today as his people and he may be your God, as he promised you and as he swore to your ancestors, to Abraham, Isaac, and Jacob." (Deuteronomy 29:12–13) Then Moses died, there on the eastern side of the Jordan River.

The land that spread out before the people was not empty. There were kingdoms and towns, with armies protecting them. It would take time and hardship for the Israelites to return to the land of their ancestors. They needed a leader. Joshua would be that leader.

Joshua had been one of Moses' helpers, and before Moses died, he laid his hands on Joshua as a way of passing on his leadership. The first big town the people came to was Jericho, and Joshua's first task was to decide how to move into this place.

> The people could see, in the distance, the city of Jericho.

The core of the Law that God gave Moses and the people at Mount Sinai was carved on stone tablets, which were stored in the Ark of the Covenant. The Israelites believed that God's power was present in the ark. They carried it with them always, obeying God's instructions about how to care for it and how to honor God's presence. On the day the people entered the Promised Land, the priests carried the ark in front of them and stopped in the middle of the Jordan River. In the same way the Red Sea divided when Moses was leading the people out of Egypt, the Jordan River opened to make a crossing for the people.

When they reached the other side of the Jordan River, the people could see, in the distance, the city of Jericho. Would the people of this city welcome them?

Joshua sent spies to see what the city and the people were like.

The two men sneaked into Jericho and came to the house of a woman named Rahab. She told them, "I know that the LORD has given you the land, that a dread of you has come upon us, and that all the inhabitants of the land tremble with fear because of you." (Joshua 2:8–9) Everyone had heard that God's power was with the Israelites—he had freed them from the Egyptians. This made the people of Jericho afraid of the Israelites. Rahab told the men that the Israelites could easily take control of Jericho. She asked that, if a battle happened, the two men would remember her and not harm her or her family. The spies agreed. They told Rahab to tie a red cord on the doorway of her house and keep her family inside with her.

The men reported back to Joshua, and he thought carefully about how to go on. On the day the people of Israel moved toward Jericho, a group of soldiers went first, and they marched around the walls of the city. They were followed by seven priests blowing trumpets made of rams' horns. They carried with them the Ark of the Covenant. They did this for six days straight, marching with the priests and the Ark but not making a sound except for the blowing of the horns.

On the seventh day, they marched again. The warriors walked, silently at first. The priests walked with the Ark of the Covenant, blowing the rams' horns. Six times around the walls they marched, and on the seventh, Joshua gave the order. "Now shout, for the LORD has given you the city." (Joshua 6:16) When the warriors shouted, the walls of Jericho crashed to the ground. As promised, Rahab and her family were protected. And the Israelites conquered the city.

This victory began many years of struggle and growth as the people of Israel settled the land. The books of Joshua and Judges tell us this story. After

Joshua died, the people were led by men and women who were called judges—such as Gideon, Deborah, and Samson.

During these years, the people of Israel learned what it meant to follow God and be his people. Over and over they learned the same lesson: when they were faithful to God and followed the way of life he had given him and worshipped him alone, they became strong. But when they forgot all that God had given them and worshipped other gods, they became weak, were defeated by other nations, and lost their freedom.

This is the story of God's people, which means it is our story, even today. When God is the center of our lives, we are who we're supposed to be. We're strong, and we become a light to the world around us.

When Joshua led the people, he reminded them of all God had done for them, and he gave them a choice. Whom are you going to serve? If you choose to serve the Lord, it's time to put away all the false gods, all the things you think will give you more happiness and peace than God does. What's your life about? Whom will you serve in your daily life?

Then Joshua said what we still say today, when we choose to live as God's people: "As for me and my household, we will serve the LORD." (Joshua 24:15)

To read more about Joshua in the Bible, go to Deuteronomy 29—31:29; and Joshua 1; 5:13—6:27.

Think Quietly: How did Jericho fall? How did Rahab help the Israelites?

Pray Together: Lord, I am here because you created me. Help me remember that today, and keep me focused on your will.

God Calls the Boy Samuel

After the time of Moses, in the city of Shiloh, a boy named Samuel lay in the darkness. It was quiet where he slept. Candles burned, and in their flickering light, gold glistened.

Shiloh was a holy place. In Shiloh was a temple, and in that temple stood the Ark of the Covenant, gilded in gold. Inside the Ark of the Covenant were the stone tablets Moses had brought down from Mount Sinai. On those stone tables were the Ten Commandments God gave his people. And it was in this holy spot that Samuel lay sleeping.

Even though Samuel was just a boy, he had this responsibility of tending the Ark of the Covenant. When he had been quite small, Samuel's mother, Hannah, brought him to this temple to live. She had prayed a long time for a child, and she promised God that she would dedicate the child God gave her to his service. Samuel was that child.

So Samuel, who was now nine or ten years old, lived with Eli, the priest in charge of worship. Eli's family kept the temple clean, helped the people when they came to offer sacrifices to God. Also, they protectd the Ark of the Covenant.

This night seemed no different from any other. But during his deep sleep, Samuel heard a voice. "Samuel!"

"Here I am," he said, and he ran to Eli, because he thought Eli had called him. But Eli had not called Samuel. He told the boy to go back to sleep, which he did.

A second time, Samuel heard that voice calling his name. Again, he rushed to Eli. But Eli had not called. "Go back to sleep!" he said.

The LORD called Samuel again, for the third time. Getting up and going to Eli, he said, "Here I am. You called me." Then Eli understood that the LORD was calling the youth. So he said to Samuel, "Go to sleep, and if you are called, reply, 'Speak, LORD, for your servant is listening.'" When Samuel went to sleep in his place, the LORD came and stood there, calling out as before: Samuel, Samuel! Samuel answered, "Speak, for your servant is listening." (1 Samuel 3:8–10)

God had a hard message for young Samuel. Eli's sons had been doing a bad job taking care of the house of the Lord. When God's people brought animals for sacrifice to the Lord, the sons of Eli kept the best parts for themselves instead of giving them to God. God told Samuel that because of these sins, Eli's family was

> During his sleep, the boy heard a voice calling, "Samuel!"

going to suffer. There was nothing they could do about it now. It was too late.

Samuel went back to sleep. In the morning, he was afraid to tell Eli what God had said. Eli told him not to be afraid. Whatever God said, Eli needed to know. "Don't hide anything," he said, and so Samuel told him everything. Eli knew that his sons had disobeyed God and hurt God's people. He had to accept the consequences of his family's actions.

"What God wants is the best for us," he said.

Sometimes we think that God won't have important things to say to us until we are grown up. The story of Samuel shows us that this isn't true. God created each of us and guides us to happiness and eternal life with him from the beginning of our lives. When we're baptized, as a baby or young child, we're made new in Jesus and anointed as priest, prophet, and king—we become part of the Body of Christ. Right then—not when we're older, but then and now—children have an important part to play in God's kingdom.

Like Samuel, we can learn to recognize when God is calling us. We can hear him in prayer time by ourselves, in prayer time at church, in the Bible, and in the lives of the saints. He calls us by name. Perhaps in a quiet place, you might hear him, too, and respond to the Lord who loves you so much: *Here I am!*

To read this whole story in the Bible, go to 1 Samuel 3:1–21.

Think Quietly: How could you find more quiet time to listen to God?

Pray Together: Lord, we know you speak to us always. Help us find more time to listen to you, and give us the courage to follow you.

David, Israel's King

When we look at the saints and great people of the Bible, we see that they don't cover up their mistakes or pretend to be someone they are not.

David has always been remembered as the greatest King of Israel, and he was, indeed, great. But he also made serious mistakes. The Bible tells the truth about David—the good and the bad.

As a boy, David worked as a shepherd. He was the youngest in his family, and no one thought of him as gifted or important in any way. But out in the wilderness, as he looked after the sheep, David became skillful with the slingshot. This is how he kept wolves and other wild animals away from the sheep.

David also composed songs and prayers, which he sang to God.

One day, Samuel the prophet came to David's father, Jesse, to secretly anoint the new King of Israel. King Saul was not obeying God, and so God would choose a new king to replace Saul. This new king would come from Jesse's family. Jesse had all his adult sons come meet Samuel, but Samuel did not choose any of them. He asked if Jesse had any more sons, and Jesse said, yes, his youngest was tending the sheep. He called David in to meet the prophet, and Samuel anointed him as Israel's next king. But David would not take his place as king right away, not while King Saul was still alive.

King Saul did not know God had anointed a new king. He knew David, though, because sometimes David would play the harp and sing for Saul. He also served as Saul's armor bearer, but at times David went home to help his father with the sheep. One day, the enemy army of the Philistines threatened to defeat Israel's army. Their leader was a giant named Goliath, and all the Israelite soldiers were afraid of him. David happened to be with the Israelite army that day because his older brothers were soldiers, and Jesse had sent David to see how they were doing. When David saw the Israelites' fear and the giant Goliath, he decided to face the enemy himself. With his slingshot and a few stones, David killed Goliath. King Saul, and the people of Israel, recognized that this young man had much courage, skill, and faith in God.

King Saul did not know that David would someday be king. But after many years and troubled times, Saul died, and David took his place as the new King of Israel. David reigned as king of God's people for many years. He had wives and children. He fought many

> Then David said, "I have sinned against the LORD."

battles. He ruled with justice. And he committed a terrible sin.

One evening, David went to the roof of his palace to relax and look over the city. Not far away, he saw a beautiful woman bathing. Her name was Bathsheba, and right away, David wanted to be with her.

But Bathsheba was married to a man named Uriah. Uriah served in David's army. In fact, Uriah was an excellent soldier. David brought Bathsheba into his palace anyway. Because he was king, he had the power to do this. We don't know how Bathsheba felt about it, but she had no choice. Her husband was away, serving in the king's army, and Bathsheba stayed with the king in his palace. Then they discovered that she was pregnant with King David's child.

David did not want to admit that he had sinned with Uriah's wife. He did not want to face Uriah. So he gave Uriah a message to take to the army's leaders on the battlefield, and Uriah obeyed. But Uriah did not know what the message said. It told the commander to put Uriah on the front lines of battle, the most dangerous place. It did not surprise anyone when Uriah was killed in battle. Now David could keep Bathsheba and make her one of his wives.

Nathan was David's court prophet and advisor. He learned about the terrible thing David had done. Because Nathan was a prophet and it was his responsibility to counsel the king, he had to go talk with King David about his sinful actions.

But Nathan was clever. He knew that if he talked to David directly about what he'd done to Bathsheba and Uriah, David would grow angry and not listen to him. So instead, Nathan told the king a story.

It was a story of two men. One man was wealthy, and he had a huge flock of sheep. Another man, a poor man, had only one lamb, which he loved very much. The wealthy man wanted to prepare a feast for a visitor. Instead of taking a lamb from his own huge flock of sheep, this rich man took the poor man's only lamb. He had it killed and cooked for the feast.

King David was outraged at his injustice—a rich man taking advantage of a poor man like that! He said to Nathan, "The man who did this deserves to die!"

Then Nathan said to David: "You are the man!"

"Thus says the LORD God of Israel: I anointed you king of Israel. . . . Why have you despised the LORD and done what is evil in his sight? You have cut down Uriah the Hittite with the sword; you took his wife as your own, and him you killed with the sword of the Ammonites."

Then David said to Nathan, "I have sinned against the LORD." Nathan answered David: "For his part, the LORD has removed your sin. You shall not die." (2 Samuel 12:7–9,13) It was the law in Israel that if a man murdered someone, he must die. God was allowing David to live. But the child he had with Bathsheba did die. She remained his wife, and they had other children, but David's selfishness and violence brought trouble to his family for many years.

David loved God and tried to serve him as king. The Bible does not hide the ways David sinned and failed. The Bible is an honest book, and those who passed on the stories we read today were inspired by the Holy Spirit to tell the truth about God and about sinful human beings who need mercy.

David was a musician, and he wrote many of the psalms that are in our Bible today. These poem-songs are just like David's life: a mix of joy and sorrow, gratitude, repentance, and praise. We pray them at Mass, and we pray them in the daily prayers—the Liturgy of the Hours—that priests, sisters, brothers, and many others pray at morning, noon, and night.

The psalms are honest about how wonderful life can be and about the many gifts God gives us. But the psalms are also honest about how painful and difficult life can be. Sometimes bad things happen because we make mistakes or wrong choices. Sometimes bad things happen, and we really don't know why. All of us need God's forgiveness and help every day. And the Psalms, like David's life, give us hope that even when we sin, God is always close, always merciful. After David repented of his sins of taking Bathsheba to his palace and killing Uriah, he wrote these words:

> Have mercy on me, God, in accord with your
>   merciful love;
>   in your abundant compassion blot out my
>   transgressions. (Psalm 51:3)

To read the whole story in the Bible, go to 1 Samuel 16:4–13; 17:1–58, and 2 Samuel 11:1—12:12.

Think Quietly: What were David's strengths? What were his weaknesses? Who helps you be honest about your strengths and weaknesses?

Pray Together: Lord, you are great and merciful. Thank you for our lives. Help us grow in virtue and love.

Solomon Asks God for Wisdom

If you were granted one wish, what would it be? What do you want more than anything? And if you got what you wanted, would it really make your life better? It takes wisdom to know what we need, not just what we want. Solomon's story is all about wisdom.

Solomon was the third King of Israel. His father was King David, who had reigned for a very long time. After David died, Solomon became the king. The country he led was growing and strong. Jerusalem was the capital of the nation, but there was no temple there, so the people offered their sacrifices to God in other places, high on the mountains.

One day, Solomon went to a place called Gideon to offer sacrifice and burn incense as he worshipped God and prepared for his new role as king. High on that mountain, Solomon slept, and God came to him in a dream. In that dream, God told Solomon, "Ask what I should give you."

Solomon could have asked for anything in the world. Anything. This is what he said to God:

"Give your servant, therefore, a listening heart to judge your people and to distinguish between good and evil. For who is able to give judgment for this vast people of yours?" (1 Kings 3:9)

Solomon asked for wisdom. He knew he would need it if he wanted to be a good leader for God's people.

So God said to him: Because you asked for this—you did not ask for a long life for yourself, nor for riches, nor for the life of your enemies—but you asked for discernment to know what is right—I now do as you request. I give you a heart so wise and understanding that there has never been anyone like you until now, nor after you will there be anyone to equal you. In addition, I give you what you have not asked for: I give you such riches and glory that among kings there will be no one like you all your days. And if you walk in my ways, keeping my statues and commandments, as David your father did, I will give you a long life. (1 Kings 3:11–14)

God answered Solomon's prayer, giving him a wise and discerning mind. As king, he would make decisions about the nation and its people and its army. But also, as king, Solomon would be a judge when people had disagreements.

Not long after this, two women came to Solomon for a judgment. They lived in the same house, and both had given birth at nearly the same time. The woman speaking to Solomon said that the other woman's baby had died in the night. The other woman had sneaked into her room and traded the babies. She took this woman's living child and laid the body of her dead baby in its place.

The women argued in front of Solomon. Each woman said that the living baby was hers. The king thought about the situation, and then he said to his servants, "Bring me a sword!"

They brought him a sword, and he gave the order: the baby would be sliced in two. Each woman would be given half the baby.

Immediately, the woman who had been speaking, who said that the babies had been switched, cried out, "Give the child to her! Let him live!" The other woman told them to go ahead and divide the child so that neither of them would have him.

Solomon knew, then, who the real mother was: the one who told him to give the baby to the other woman so that the child could live. A mother would love her child enough to give him up rather than see him killed. So Solomon gave the child to his mother.

Solomon used his wisdom to serve God and God's people. He built a beautiful, rich temple to honor God in Jerusalem, a fitting house for the Ark of the Covenant.

But as was the case so many times in the story of God's people, Solomon did not remain faithful. The kingdom grew, and Solomon became wealthy and powerful, far richer than any king before him. He had many wives. Some of them were Israelites, but many of them were not. They came from other nations, and they brought their own "gods"—idols—with them into Solomon's palace. As time went by, Solomon became used to being rich and doing whatever he wanted. He began to forget that all his gifts came from God. Solomon began to honor the gods of his wives and even built temples for them so his wives could offer sacrifices and incense.

Solomon was the last king to reign over a united nation of Israel. He began his reign in faith and humility, begging God to give him wisdom and understanding. But then Solomon forgot the love of God, who had given him life and wisdom. Solomon forgot that God had created the whole world and called the nation Israel to be a light to the nations, freeing them from superstition, fear, and injustice.

Solomon's son, Rehoboam, became king, and during his reign, the kingdom of Israel split apart. Perhaps if Solomon had not become distracted by wealth and power, he could have passed on wisdom to his son.

> Solomon used his wisdom to serve God and God's people.

Jesus once said that it is harder for a rich man to get into heaven than it is for a camel to go through the eye of a needle. He wanted us to know that when we feel satisfied by the things of this world, we can begin to think that our wealth, talents, and success are really all we need to be happy. We forget that we need God every day.

This happened to Solomon, and it can happen to any of us. So what is our prayer? Like Solomon, we keep praying for wisdom. And we live by the wisdom God gives us, so that we can see ourselves honestly and remember that God alone saves us.

To read more of Solomon's story in the Bible, go to 1 Kings 3:5–14, 16–28 and 11:1–13.

Think Quietly: Why did Solomon pray for wisdom? How did Solomon fall from wisdom? What tempts us to forget God?

Pray Together: God of wisdom, help us live in understanding and truth always.

Jesus Is Baptized

We don't know much about Jesus' life between his birth
and his public ministry. We know that he grew up in
Nazareth, in Galilee. We think that Joseph died before
Jesus began his ministry because Joseph is not
mentioned in the Gospel stories of Jesus as an adult.
Also, we don't see Joseph at Jesus' crucifixion or
burial—we see his mother, Mary, at both. Before he
dies on the cross, Jesus tells his mother that the
Apostle John is now her son, and he tells John that
Mary is now his mother. This was Jesus' way of making
certain his elderly mother was cared for. He would not
have done this if Joseph had still been alive.

Luke tells us one story about the child Jesus. When
he was about twelve years old, the family traveled to

Jerusalem to celebrate the Passover, as they did every year. They traveled with others in a big group, and after the festival, they all began the journey back to Nazareth. After a day, Mary and Joseph noticed that Jesus was not with them. They thought he was with other families in the group, but no one had seen him.

So Mary and Joseph went back to Jerusalem, where they looked—and looked—for Jesus. Finally, after three days of searching, they found him in the temple. Jesus was listening to the Scripture teachers and asking questions. Those who listened to him speak were amazed at his wisdom.

His parents were astonished too, and Mary told him how worried they had been. Jesus responded, "Why were you looking for me? Did you not know that I must be in my Father's house?" (Luke 2:49)

They returned to Nazareth. Mary remembered and thought about all these things, and Jesus continued to grow up.

Years later, when Jesus was an adult, his cousin John was living in the wilderness near the Jordan River. He was depending on God alone, wearing camel skins for clothing, and eating only what he could find in the wild: locusts and honey.

John preached there and baptized people who wanted to change their lives. He was doing just what the angel Gabriel told Zechariah he would do: prepare the way for God's Chosen One. John told his listeners that he was baptizing with water, but the one coming after him would baptize them with the Holy Spirit. People came from all around the region to listen to him. They felt sorry for the ways they had wandered from God, and so they let John baptize them as a sign of God's mercy that gives us clean hearts that are ready to change.

One day, Jesus came to the river too. John saw him. He told those around him that this man was the

Lamb of God, who would take away the sins of the world. In fact, John did not want to baptize Jesus—he said that Jesus should baptize *him*. Jesus insisted, saying, "Allow it now; for thus it is fitting for us to fulfill all righteousness." . . . After Jesus was baptized, he came up from the water and behold, the heavens were opened [for him], and he saw the Spirit of God descending like a dove [and] coming upon him. And a voice came from the heavens, saying, "This is my beloved Son, with whom I am well pleased."

(Matthew 3:16–17)

Jesus' mission was clear. He was God's Son, the Lamb of God, and through his sacrifice, the sins of the world would be forgiven. For centuries, God's people had offered the best of their crops and animals to God as a way of telling him they were sorry for their sins. They did this again and again, for years and years. But Jesus would take on all the sins, and what had been broken by our first parents' no would be made right by the yes of sacrifice of the Lamb of God on the cross, once and for all.

When we are baptized, we are washed clean of our Original Sin and joined to the Body of Christ, the Church. We become new creatures in Christ! But Jesus didn't sin. So why was he baptized?

As Jesus plunged into the waters of the river, the waters that sinners entered, he joined us in this earthly life, and then he brought us up out of the water to new life. The waters of Baptism are like the Father's will. Under the hand of John, God's prophet, Jesus submits himself to the Father's will, and from heaven the Father sends a sign. It's a sign the Apostles will witness at the Transfiguration. It's a sign Jesus lives out when he's praying in the Garden of Gethsemane.

It's the mission Jesus told his parents about when they found him in the temple.

Of all the details and stories we could know about Jesus' life, his baptism tells us the most important part: his life was a mission of love for us. He lived and died for us. And through him, we can be with God forever!

> "This is my beloved Son, with whom I am well pleased."

To read the whole story in the Bible, go to Matthew 3:13–17 and John 1:19–34.

Think Quietly: Why was Jesus baptized? What does your Baptism give you?

Pray Together: Jesus, you are the Lamb of God. May the grace of our Baptism help us live the Father's will.

Jesus at the Wedding in Cana

Jesus, his mother, Mary, and some of his friends had been invited to a wedding in a town called Cana. During Jesus' time, a wedding was a huge celebration that might last for a week.

Jesus attended this wedding after he had been baptized by his cousin John in the Jordan River. Jesus had not yet begun to preach and teach and heal. No one really knew about his mission yet. He was just the carpenter's son from Nazareth, there at a wedding feast with his family and friends.

During the celebrations, Mary learned that the family had a problem. They had run out of wine.

The man who was getting married—the bridegroom—was responsible for providing all the food and drink for the wedding feast. Imagine if you were that bridegroom or part of his family and you *ran out of wine for the party!* It would be a disaster! This would cause so much embarrassment for the bridegroom's family. Mary knew this. So she turned to her son Jesus and said, "They have no wine."

Jesus' answer to his mother about this problem is a little confusing. He told her, "My hour has not yet come." Later, Jesus would heal a paralyzed man in front of many people. He would feed thousands with a few fish and loaves of bread. He would rise from the dead and send his friends out to tell the whole world about it. But here at the wedding feast, he would give a different kind of sign. It would certainly be a sign of his power, love, and the happiness that God wants to share with all of us. But it would also be a quieter kind of sign that would help the people in need right then and there.

> Mary told the servants to do whatever Jesus told them to do.

Mary told the servants nearby to do whatever Jesus told them to do.

There were empty wine jars at the party, but Jesus did not use them. Now there were six stone water jars there for Jewish ceremonial washings, each holding twenty to thirty gallons. (John 2:6)

The Jewish people didn't want anything in their lives to come between them and God's holy presence. To help themselves prepare for praying or going into holy places, the people washed their hands and faces, and even their feet. It was a way of being clean and ready for God's holy presence. Jesus directed the servants to these jars used for ceremonial washing.

Jesus told them, "Fill the jars with water." So they filled them to the brim. Then he told them, "Draw some out now, and take it to the headwaiter." (John 2:7–8)

The servants filled the jars with water. Then Jesus told the servants to give some of it to the headwaiter to taste. We can imagine that the servants were not eager to serve the headwaiter plain water! But they did as Jesus instructed.

And when the headwaiter tasted the water that had become wine, without knowing where it came from (although the servers who had drawn the water knew), the headwaiter called the bridegroom and said to him, "Everyone serves good wine first, and then when people have drunk freely, an inferior one; but you have kept the good wine until now." Jesus did this as the beginning of his signs in Cana in Galilee and so revealed his glory, and his disciples began to believe in him. (John 2:9–11)

Jesus didn't turn water into this new wine at the wedding feast to show off. His miracle was a sign of love. It was a sign for the people in need at the wedding. It was also a sign for us now.

Whenever we have problems—big ones or small ones—Jesus wants us to bring them to him. Mary is there for us too, waiting. We can, like the people at the feast, take our troubles to her, trusting that she'll pray for us, helping us know that we will find the solution to our problems by doing what Jesus tells us to do.

Jesus wants to share with us his life and love. He wants us to come to the celebration that will last forever. That celebration starts right now, because Jesus has come to earth, he lives among us, and he shares his life with us in the feast.

To read the whole story in the Bible, go to John 2:1—12.

Think Quietly: How was Jesus' miracle at Cana a sign of who he is? How did Mary help with the problem at the wedding feast? How does Mary help us?

Pray Together: Jesus, we bring our troubles to you. We will do what you say, and find peace.

Jesus Calls His First Disciples

Jesus had entered the waters of baptism at the Jordan River. He had gone into the desert for forty days to pray, where the Devil had tried to tempt him.

He entered the synagogue in Nazareth, where he had grown up. Many were gathered in the synagogue, a place of study and prayer. Jesus stood up to take his turn reading from Scripture, and from the scroll that was handed to him, he read from the prophet Isaiah:

> The Spirit of the Lord is upon me,
>   because he has anointed me
>   to bring glad tidings to the poor. (Luke 4:18)

It was the custom for the person who read the Scripture aloud to talk about what it might mean. Jesus explained that this prophecy from Isaiah was being fulfilled right then and there. What a shocking thing to say! This prophecy was about the Messiah—was Jesus claiming to be the Messiah? Jesus, the carpenter's son? They had watched him grow up. They knew his mother and father. And now he was speaking blasphemy, which was the worst kind of sin. The people didn't want anything to do with Jesus now. In anger, they drove him out of the synagogue. Some even wanted to kill him.

Jesus made clear who he was, to those who could understand. From the beginning, this made some people angry. But it made others hopeful.

Soon after Jesus began teaching, preaching, and healing, he came to the Sea of Galilee. Already, many people were coming to hear Jesus and seek his help. It became so crowded that Jesus decided to get in one of the fishing boats, go a little way from the shore, and preach from the boat.

The boat Jesus chose belonged to a fisherman named Simon. When Jesus finished teaching, he told Simon to take the boat out further and start fishing. Simon told Jesus that they had already been fishing all night and hadn't caught anything. Why go out again? But if Jesus really wanted them to, they would go.

When they had done this, they caught a great number of fish and their nets were tearing. They signaled to their partners in the other boat to come to help them. (Luke 5:6–7)

Simon knew then that Jesus was different from other teachers. He had just performed a miracle right in front of them. Jesus was a holy man. When Simon Peter saw this, he fell at the knees of Jesus and said, "Depart from me, Lord, for I am a sinful man." (Luke 5:8)

But Jesus didn't go away. He told Simon that if he came along with him, he would make him a fisher of men.

Simon said yes. And so did his brother Andrew and their partners, James and John. All four left their lives behind at that moment to follow Jesus.

Simon and Andrew were from a town called Bethsaida. Jesus met another man there named Philip and said to him, "Follow me."

Philip immediately went to his friend Nathanael and told him about this Jesus of Nazareth. He was the one they had been waiting for—the one the prophets had written about.

Nathanael couldn't believe this. He said to Philip, "Can anything good come out of Nazareth?" Everyone knew that Nazareth was an unimportant place.

Philip said to him, "Come and see." (John 1:46)

Jesus saw the two coming, and he said of Nathanael, "Here is truly an Israelite in whom there is no deceit!" He meant that Nathanael was honest and true and said what he thought. That was a good thing!

Then Jesus met a tax collector named Matthew, a Jewish man hired by the Romans to collect taxes from his own people. Tax collectors were considered sinners by other Jews. If you wanted to be close to God, you would not have any contact with a tax collector.

Jesus saw Matthew sitting at his place of business, doing a job that made his Jewish neighbors despise and avoid him.

"Follow me," Jesus said to the outcast. And Matthew did just that.

Jesus called, and people answered. He invited them to leave their everyday lives and follow him. Many did. As Jesus continued to travel around the countryside, preaching and teaching, his group of followers grew. Hundreds of men and women heard Jesus and were healed by him. They understood that if they followed Jesus, they would discover a different sort of life than they had ever known. With him, there was mercy and hope.

The twelve Apostles were those Jesus called to work with him closely. They would lead and teach in his name, just as priests today are called to do by the Church. The twelve Apostles were the **first bishops to** shepherd in Jesus' name, which is why our bishops today are called "successors of the Apostles" and each carries a staff that looks like a shepherd's crook. "Follow me," Jesus said to all kinds of people. "Follow me," he says to you and me. We all are called by Jesus to bring the Good News to our friends and neighbors. We are all called to be part of the Body of Christ.

> "Follow me," Jesus said to Philip.

When we are living our ordinary lives, Jesus calls us. When we are far away from God, and even when we think there is no way back, Jesus reaches out and calls us to follow him.

Jesus sees who we are and who we can be. He sees the ways we can love and serve God and his people. Living in communion with Jesus, we can be transformed if we listen for his voice: *Follow me.*

To read the whole story in the Bible, go to John 1:35–51 and Luke 5:1–11.

Think Quietly: What were the Apostles like? How did saying yes to Jesus change their lives?

Pray Together: Jesus, may our hearts be open to your call.

Jesus Heals

During his time on earth, Jesus preached. He taught
and told stories and parables. He shared God's mercy.
He reached out to people others had rejected. He
prayed, calmed the storms, and broke bread and
shared it.

Jesus also healed people. The Gospels are full of
memories of the many people Jesus touched and
healed: a man with a withered hand. Blind men. A
woman who suffered from bleeding. Sick children.
Peter's mother-in-law. Jesus even healed people who
were possessed by demons.

When Jesus was traveling between Samaria and
Galilee one day, ten lepers found him. In those days,
people who suffered from leprosy could not live in the

villages or towns. No one knew how to cure this disease, and people were afraid of catching it. They also believed that a horrible disease such as leprosy was a sign that God did not accept that person. It was almost like having a curse. Such people were called unclean. If you were in close contact with people who had leprosy, that made you unclean, too.

So these lepers, who could not take part in ordinary life, were condemned for being outside God's favor. They found Jesus but stayed far away from him, and they called out, "Jesus, Master! Have pity on us!" (Luke 17:13)

> The Gospels tell of the many people Jesus touched and healed.

Jesus told them to go back into the town and show themselves to the priest. A priest was the only person who could examine them and see if the leprosy was gone. And if it was, the priest would allow the person back into the community.

On the way to see the priest, each leper discovered that he had been healed. Out of the ten lepers, only one returned to Jesus. He raced back, praising God, threw himself at Jesus' feet, and thanked him. This one person happened to be a Samaritan, not part of the Jewish community.

Jesus said in reply, "Ten were cleansed, were they not? Where are the other nine? Has none but this foreigner returned to give thanks to God?" Then he said to him, "Stand up and go; your faith has saved you." (Luke 17:17–19)

Another time, Jesus was going to Capernaum, the town near the Sea of Galilee that was his home as an adult. A Roman centurion heard that Jesus was coming and sent some Jewish friends of his with a request. These friends told Jesus that even though the centurion was not a Jew, he was kind to the Jewish people and even helped them build their synagogue.

But now the centurion's servant was sick and close to death. Could Jesus come?

Jesus agreed, and as they walked toward the centurion's home, some other friends of the centurion met Jesus with a message. The centurion wanted Jesus to know that he, too, was a man who had authority over others. When he gave soldiers or servants jobs to do, he knew they would do them. Jesus had authority too—the centurion knew this. He had faith that even if Jesus didn't come to his home, his power would still heal the servant. He said, "Lord, do not trouble yourself, for I am not worthy to have you enter under my roof. . . . But say the word and let my servant be healed." (Luke 7:6–7)

Jesus was amazed. Once again, an unexpected person, an outsider, had shown faith. And, of course, the centurion's slave was healed at that moment.

In Jesus' time, health was a sign of blessing, and sickness was the opposite. But with Jesus, the sick encountered something new. He healed them and made them whole as a sign of what life in God's kingdom was like. In God's kingdom we are at peace, inside and out. When Jesus gave sight to the blind, made the lame walk and the deaf hear, he was fulfilling God's promise of what life with him is like.

The sick could meet God and experience his power even while they were in pain, while they were sick, while they were outcasts in their community. They were not excluded from God's blessing. In their sickness, which others said cut them off from God's blessing, they were blessed.

When Jesus preached the Beatitudes, he said this clearly. As he gathered the crowds around him, he told them what it meant to be blessed and how we know we are close to God—and it seemed to be quite different from anything they had ever heard before.

Blessed are the poor in spirit . . . blessed are those who mourn . . . blessed are the meek . . . blessed are those who are persecuted. . . .

In our own suffering, we can feel alone, sad, and frustrated. A little cold can get us down, a bad problem that won't go away can make us feel different from others. If we are seriously ill in body or mind, it can be hard to find people who understand what we are going through.

This is where Jesus meets us. We're not alone. He meets us in the Sacrament of the Anointing of the Sick. He meets us in the gift of himself in the Eucharist. He meets us in the prayers that others pray for us, every time we, as the Body of Christ, pray for the sick and suffering. He's with us in our suffering because he knows suffering himself.

In faith, we come to Jesus as the centurion did, trusting him. In gratitude, we return as the Samaritan leper did, knowing that Jesus is with us in our suffering. With open hearts, we live that mystery: in our brokenness, we can know God's peace.

To read more about these events in the Bible, go to Luke 7:1–10; Luke 17:11–19; Luke 6:20–26; and Matthew 5:2–12.

Think Quietly: Why do you think the other lepers might not have returned to thank Jesus? Why did the centurion trust Jesus? How is Jesus present with you in suffering?

Pray Together: Jesus, we pray for all those who are sick. May they know you in their suffering, and find peace.

ORDINARY
TIME

Parables of Seeds and Other Growing Things

Jesus knew that stories are the best way to teach. Jesus used a kind of story called a parable. A parable is a story that helps us understand one thing by comparing it to another. Parables are usually short, but that doesn't mean they are simple. Jesus' parables help us in different ways at different times.

When Jesus preached and taught, he was talking to ordinary people who lived in a certain time and place: first-century Israel. So his stories were about things those people would understand. The characters are farmers, travelers, judges and widows, brothers and businessmen, rich and poor. In Jesus' parables, people are planting, cleaning, building, feasting, spending money, going to court, building houses, and managing businesses.

Jesus' parables remind us to look for signs of God in every part of life, even in the dusty corners of our house, the dirt of our gardens, or our daily routines. These parables also show us something about the Kingdom of God. They challenge us to think about where we stand in God's kingdom. Are we preparing? Are we ready? Is it the most important thing in our life? Are we open to the mercy and justice of God's kingdom? And are we ready *right now*?

Many people Jesus talked to knew all about plants and farming, so Jesus often told parables about seeds, fields, and plants. Like this one:

A man went out to plant seeds. And as he sowed some seed fell on the path, and birds came and ate it up. Some fell on rocky ground, where it had little soil. It sprang up at once because the soil was not deep, and when the sun rose it was scorched, and it withered for lack of roots. Some seed fell among thorns, and the thorns grew up and choked it. But some seed fell on rich soil and produced fruit, a hundred or sixty or thirtyfold. (Matthew 13:4–8)

Usually, Jesus didn't explain his parables, but he explained this one to the disciples. He said that the seed is God's Word: the good news of the Kingdom of God. If it comes to someone who won't understand it, it's as if it were tossed on the path and evil comes along and snatches it away.

The rocky ground is the heart of a person who is happy to hear the Good News at first, but once trouble comes, he or she lets the good fruit wither.

> God plants his kingdom in ways that look small to us.

The thorns, Jesus said, are the cares of the world. When someone lets earthly worries dominate his or her life, it's like thorns choking out the Word of God.

But there is that good soil, isn't there? That's our heart when we are open and try to understand the seed that's sown in it. That's our life when we accept the seed of God's Word and let it flourish—and it does, and it bears fruit in our lives.

Jesus tells us that we could see what the Kingdom of Heaven was like by thinking about someone coming in the middle of the night and trying to ruin a field by planting weeds among the wheat. The owner's servants asked him if he wanted them to uproot the weeds, and he surprised them by saying no. He told them to wait until harvest. Then they would take it all up together and separate the good from the bad. Life in this world, Jesus told his Apostles later, is full of those who follow God and those who don't. It's up to God to separate them at the end of the world, and he will.

One of the smallest seeds in the world is that of a mustard plant. It's tiny, just a speck. Jesus told a very short parable about this plant: he said that the Kingdom of God is like one of those mustard seeds, which is tiny, but it grows into a plant that's so large, many birds can come and make a home in its branches.

God plants his kingdom in ways that look small to us, but it grows big enough to take care of us and give us a spiritual home.

Jesus told a parable about a person who knew that a treasure was buried somewhere in a field. He sold everything he had so he could buy that field, just for the treasure. This treasure was worth his whole life.

Jesus told another parable about someone who planted seeds at night. In the morning he wakes up to a huge harvest, with the miracle of plants all around him. Their growth is a surprising, delightful mystery.

What is the Kingdom of God like? It is surprising. It can seem hidden in the busy lives we lead in the world. It is more important than anything else.

Through his parables, Jesus makes it clear that God's kingdom is *God's* kingdom. He's in charge. We're part of it. We're invited to help spread the Good News of that kingdom. But we can't control it. Also, it's not our job to decide who is in the kingdom and who isn't. And it's not our job to decide how God works or where God should be.

We watch, we listen, we care for God's life in us, and we hope—and we let God's kingdom grow!

To read the whole story in the Bible, go to Matthew 13:1–53.

Think Quietly: What seeds has God planted in your life? What kind of soil is your heart?

Pray Together: God, reign with love in our hearts. May we never get in the way of the spread of your kingdom of love.

Parables on the Spiritual Life

One day, Jesus' disciples saw him praying and asked him to teach them. John the Baptist taught his disciples how to pray. Could Jesus do the same?

Jesus taught them this prayer: "Our Father . . ."

Jesus wasn't just teaching his disciples a prayer to learn and repeat. He was teaching them *how* to pray no matter what words they used.

When you pray, Jesus was saying, put God first. God is our Father, his name is holy, he reigns on heaven and earth, and we live so that his will be done, because he is Lord.

Then, after focusing your prayer on God, bring your needs to that loving Father! We know who God is and what he can do, so we ask him!

Don't be afraid to pray, Jesus told his disciples. Don't be afraid to ask God for anything. God loves you and will give you what you need, whether you know what you need or not. God will help you in the way that's best for you.

After all, Jesus said, if someone comes to the door of a neighbor in the middle of the night asking for bread for a visitor, is that neighbor going to lock the doors and say no? He might at first, but if the first person is persistent, he's sure to get out of bed and help.

He told another parable about a woman who had to go to court and ask a judge for help. This judge was not good or fair, and he did not want to help the woman. But the woman wouldn't give up. She kept coming back to the judge again and again, and finally, he gave in. If an unjust judge will finally relent, Jesus said, surely God, who is just and who loves us, will hear us when we're in need.

Think about parents and children, Jesus says. "What father among you would hand his son a snake when he asks for a fish? Or hand him a scorpion when he asks for an egg? If you then . . . know how to give good gifts to your children, how much more will the Father in heaven give the holy Spirit to those who ask him?" (Luke 11:11–13)

We are searching, growing, and seeking a purpose for our lives. Really, we are seeking for God. Every minute of every day is part of this journey to God, and prayer is the time we focus on our good desires and open our hearts to God's generosity. We can do this with confidence; we can do this every day because we know something important: God is seeking us, too.

> Don't be afraid to pray, Jesus told his disciples.

Jesus tells parables about this. He was being questioned by Pharisees and others who didn't understand why Jesus spent time with all sorts of people, including people who were considered sinners and unclean. He didn't just treat them politely and walk away. He welcomed them and shared meals with them. Wasn't he worried about being around people who were not living the right way?

To answer this question, Jesus told a story.

It was a simple story about a shepherd. But he told it in a way that helped the people criticizing him come closer to God. He wasn't just teaching them a new idea. He was inviting them into God's merciful heart.

"What man among you having a hundred sheep and losing one of them would not leave the ninety-nine in the desert and go after the lost one until he finds it?" (Luke 15:4)

For that is what a shepherd would do. He wouldn't want any of his sheep to be lost. He would risk everything to search for the one lost sheep, and he would rejoice when he found it.

Jesus then told a parable about a woman who had ten silver coins and lost one. His listeners understood that Jesus was talking about a wedding necklace, which had ten coins. A woman would be desperate to find such a lost coin. If one of the coins were missing, this symbol of joy and love would be incomplete, so of course, the woman would sweep her house until she found it. And when she found it, she would have a celebration!

And so we come to the Lord in prayer, seeking him. Sometimes we use our own words, and sometimes we use the words of prayers that other people have written. We use words from the Bible. We pray the Rosary, we pray psalms, and we pray at Mass. We are seeking God. We are being quiet and listening. We are praising him. We are asking questions and trusting that he will give us everything we need. And we can come to that place of prayer every day, knowing that the Lord wants us to come. We may feel lost, but we never are, for God is seeking us, his precious lambs, his treasure. He rejoices when we are found and when we open our hearts to him!

To read these parables in the Bible, go to Luke 11:1–13; Luke 15:1–10; and Luke 18:1–8.

Think Quietly: What are my favorite kinds of prayer? How can I find time to pray more? How can I make my prayer be more like the way Jesus teaches me to pray?

Pray Together: Our Father . . .

ORDINARY
TIME

The Story of the Good Samaritan

People were watching Jesus. They were listening to him. People were asking questions.

One of these was a lawyer. He was an expert in the Jewish Law, which was called the Torah. This lawyer helped others understand how to live according to God's Law: what food they could eat, whether a certain activity was permitted on the Sabbath, or how people in a community or family should treat one another.

His question to Jesus was simple: "Teacher, what must I do to inherit eternal life?" Jesus said to him, "What is written in the law? How do you read it?" He said in reply, "You shall love the Lord, your God, with all your heart, with all your being, with all your strength, and with all your mind, and your neighbor as yourself." (Luke 10:25–27)

The lawyer knew these words by heart. Any Jewish person who paid attention to faith would memorize this Scripture. It's from the Book of Deuteronomy and part of a prayer called the *Shema*. Even today, many Jewish people recite the Shema first thing in the morning and the last thing at night.

Well then, Jesus said, there is your answer. Love God and your neighbor, and you will live.

For some reason, the lawyer was not satisfied. Luke tells us that he wanted to "justify himself," and he had another question. "Who is my neighbor?"

The lawyer probably thought he knew the answer to this one, too. In his tradition, it was clear who a neighbor was: a member of your family or someone in your Jewish community who also lived by the Law. A neighbor was not a foreigner or a person who worshipped other gods. It certainly wasn't your enemy.

That might have been what the lawyer expected Jesus to say, but once again, Jesus didn't give a direct, easy answer. He told this parable.

There was a man walking from the heights of Jerusalem to the town of Jericho down in a valley. This eighteen-mile journey was along a road lined with large rocky areas and caves, perfect for robbers to hide in. Before the man could reach Jericho, some robbers jumped out and attacked him. They robbed him and even took his clothes. They left him badly wounded at the side of the road.

As he lay there, helpless and seriously injured, a priest of the Jerusalem temple came along. He saw the hurt man lying at the side of the road. The priest crossed to the other side.

A Levite came next. The Levites had the job of taking care of the temple. This man, too, passed on the other side of the road.

Why didn't they stop? Jesus doesn't explain, but we can guess. Perhaps they thought it was a trap—that the man was pretending to be hurt to draw them closer so his friends could rob them. Or perhaps they were concerned with the Law. Touching a dead body made a priest and Levite unclean. If the priest were on his way to Jerusalem to serve at the temple, and if he touched a dead body, he would have to go through rituals that would take a lot of time to be made clean again. This was the Law. The Torah lawyer would know this very well. Maybe he would even see himself in their place.

A third man came along the road. He wasn't a priest or a Levite. He wasn't even Jewish. He was a Samaritan. A Samaritan was about the worst person Jesus could have put into this story because he was telling the story to a group of Jewish people. The people of Samaria thought of themselves as followers of God, but through the years they had made their own traditions, which were different from Jewish practices. To Jewish people, Samaritans were fake. They pretended to be God's people, but they had left the true way of following God. Jews avoided Samaritans.

Jewish people of this time would not choose a Samaritan to be the hero of the story. But here he was in Jesus' parable, the only person to stop and help the suffering man.

Moved with pity, the Samaritan soothed the man's wounds with oil and cleaned them with wine, and he put bandages on them. He put the man on his own donkey and took him to an inn where he could rest and get better. The Samaritan even stayed the night to be sure the wounded man would be all right. The next day, the Samaritan gave money to the innkeeper and told him to care for the wounded man. On his return trip, the Samaritan would pay back the innkeeper for anything more he had spent to care for the man.

Then Jesus asked, "Which of these three, in your opinion, was neighbor to the robbers' victim?" He answered, "The one who treated him with mercy." Jesus said to him, "Go and do likewise." (Luke 10:36–37)

When it comes to love, mercy, and charity, Jesus tells us that everyone is a neighbor. Many early Christians listened to this parable and heard the challenge to love all people, and it's a challenge we live out in our Corporal and Spiritual Works of Mercy.

The early Christians also saw symbolism in this parable. The man was each one of us on our journey through life. We were created from a heavenly source—Jerusalem on high—and are making our way through the lower places of the world, which is like Jericho. On the way, we have been attacked and hurt by sin. The old ways can't help us, but Jesus—the outsider, who many reject—*can* help us, and he does. He heals the wounds of our soul with the sacraments, and he carries us to the safe place of the Church. He leaves the wounded there, in the care of the Church—which means in our care—until he comes again.

> Jews in Jesus' day would not choose a Samaritan to be the hero of the story.

To read the whole story in the Bible, go to Luke 10:25–37.

Think Quietly: Who is my neighbor? How does my faith in Jesus help me treat all people as my neighbor? How is Jesus like the Good Samaritan?

Pray Together: Jesus, you come to us and take care of our hurts. Help us do this for other people.

Jesus and the Storms

Sometimes, on a perfectly peaceful summer day, a
storm can come. And it can happen quickly, too. The
sky fills with dark clouds, and thunder shakes the air.
Then the lightning comes, and a heavy downpour of
rain. A storm can do a lot of damage. It can knock down
trees and branches. It can cause floods.

And when you're in a boat on the water, a storm
can be especially scary.

Jesus and his friends were in a boat on the Sea of
Galilee. The Sea of Galilee is a big lake with the Jordan
River running into one side of it and out the other.
Mountains stand near the Sea of Galilee, and
sometimes cold air rushes down from those mountains
and meets the warm air and water from the lake, and

the collision of cold and warm air can produce terrible, sudden storms.

That's what happened that night. News of Jesus had spread. More and more people had heard about his teaching and that he was healing the sick, so crowds were coming to see Jesus, hear him teach, and be touched by him for healing.

Jesus said it was time to get in the boat and go across to the other side of the lake. As he and the Apostles made their way across the water, Jesus slept, weary from all his time ministering to the crowds. In the sky, clouds gathered, and the wind started to blow. A huge storm developed. But Jesus kept sleeping.

> "Save us, Lord!" they cried. "We're going to die!"

The storm continued. Waves started to crash into the boat. They were nowhere near shore. What would they do? Finally, the Apostles woke up Jesus.

"Save us, Lord!" they cried. "We're going to die!"

He [Jesus] woke up, rebuked the wind, and said to the sea, "Quiet! Be still!" The wind ceased and there was great calm. Then he asked them, "Why are you terrified? Do you not yet have faith?" (Mark 4:39–40)

The Apostles were amazed. They had been with Jesus for a few weeks. They had heard him preach and teach. Not long before this, they saw him heal a leper, the servant of a centurion, and Peter's mother-in-law.

They had seen Jesus do great things, but this was a different kind of miracle. They wondered: what sort of man was this that even the winds and the sea obeyed him?

This wasn't the only time Jesus' friends were caught in a storm on the Sea of Galilee. On another night, Jesus had stayed on shore, and they were out on the boat. A storm blew up, and for hours and hours they worked and struggled, trying to reach safety. Sometime between three and six o'clock in the morning, they looked out into the rainy, windy darkness and saw someone on the water, coming near them. They were terrified because they thought it was a ghost.

But it was Jesus, walking straight through the storm on the water. "Don't be afraid," he said to them.

Peter called out to Jesus. "Lord, if it is you, command me to come to you on the water." He said, "Come." Peter got out of the boat and began to walk on the water toward Jesus. But when he saw how [strong] the wind was he became frightened; and, beginning to sink, he cried out, "Lord, save me!" Immediately Jesus stretched out his hand and caught him, and said to him, "O you of little faith, why did you doubt?" (Matthew 14:28–31)

They climbed into the boat, and the winds and storm stopped. The Apostles said that surely Jesus was the Son of God.

Storms come up all the time in our lives, and not just outside in rain and wind. Our family life can be stormy. School can make us feel like we're drowning and we need someone to rescue us. When we are angry at ourselves or don't feel happy about ourselves, it can feel as if we're being beaten up by a strong wind. These kinds of storms, just like rainstorms, can frighten and hurt us.

Jesus never promised his friends there wouldn't be any storms. Sometimes we get the idea that having faith means that we shouldn't have trouble anymore, but that's just not true.

Storms will come, but here in the boat with us is Jesus. The Apostles got frightened and anxious because they were paying more attention to the storm than they were to Jesus, who was right there with them in the boat. They knew he could help—that's why they woke him up. But they still doubted, just a little bit, and so they were scared. When they were out in the storm without Jesus, they weren't looking for him, so they didn't recognize him at first. Then Peter, even with Jesus in sight, began to listen to the wind more than he kept his eyes on Jesus. And so he sank.

But Jesus was right there. Our storms can threaten to overwhelm us, too. They're noisy and powerful, and we can think that the storm is the most real thing in our life, and that nothing else exists outside it. We think that our life is nothing but that storm.

Jesus is with us, though, and there are ways to help ourselves remember that. If we have memorized prayers, even short ones, we can have them in our mind and heart to whisper when things get hard: *Jesus, I trust in you*. If we wear a religious medal or crucifix around our neck, when we get scared in stormy times, we can touch it and remember the truth: Jesus is with us. Jesus will always be with us, and he's stronger than any storm, inside or out.

To read the whole story in the Bible, go to Matthew 14:22–33 and Mark 4:35–41.

Think Quietly: What are some storms that you've been through? How can you help yourself remember that Jesus is always with you in the storms?

Pray Together: Jesus, you are the Son of God, Lord of heaven and earth. Give us peace in our storms.

Jesus Feeds a Multitude with Loaves and Fishes

Jesus and his disciples traveled around Galilee, preaching and healing the sick. Jesus told his friends that they should rest awhile. To find some privacy and be able to relax, they got into boats and went out on the Sea of Galilee. When they came back to shore, they saw that news about Jesus had spread. Crowds were coming to meet them.

Jesus saw them. Hundreds, even thousands of people from all the nearby towns, coming to be close to him. He was moved with compassion because to him they looked like sheep without a shepherd.

It was getting late, and, of course, people were hungry. The Apostles told Jesus to send the crowds back to the villages so they could buy food for themselves.

He [Jesus] said to them in reply, "Give them some food yourselves." But they said to him, "Are we to buy two hundred days' wages worth of food and give it to them to eat?" He asked them, "How many loaves do you have? Go and see." And when they had found out they said, "Five loaves and two fish." (Mark 6:37–38)

Jesus told the Apostles to tell the crowds to sit down, and so they spread out on the hillside: women, men, boys, and girls.

Jesus took the bread. He looked up to heaven. He gave thanks. He blessed the bread and broke it and gave it to the disciples to give to the people. He then gave out the fish to the people. Everyone in that crowd ate until they were full! Afterward, they collected the leftovers, and there was so much food that it filled twelve baskets.

Later, Jesus spoke to some of them about what he had shared with them. He had gone back to Capernaum, but many followed him there. They found him and talked to him in the synagogue. Jesus told them that they were interested in him not because the miraculous meal was a sign of God's power but because their stomachs were filled. They shouldn't be working for food that satisfies for only a while, but for the food that will nourish them forever.

Jesus said to them, "I am the bread of life; whoever comes to me will never hunger, and whoever believes in me will never thirst." (John 6:35)

What Jesus was saying was hard to understand. It was a little upsetting, too. The people knew who Jesus was: the son of a carpenter from Nazareth. Who was he to say that he was the bread from heaven?

Jesus kept explaining. God had given the Israelites manna—food from heaven—in the wilderness, but this food satisfied only for a little while. Jesus was the bread from heaven, and his flesh would give eternal life.

That was an odd thing to say! Those listening started to wonder. Was Jesus saying he was giving people his flesh to eat?

"Whoever eats my flesh and drinks my blood has eternal life, and I will raise him on the last day. For my flesh is true food, and my blood is true drink." (John 6:54–55)

Well, these words were strange, and people thought Jesus might not be a prophet or the Messiah after all. This was a hard teaching, they said. Who could accept it? Many of the listeners left then. Even some of the disciples who had been following Jesus left.

Jesus then said to the Twelve [apostles], "Do you also want to leave?" Simon Peter answered him, "Master, to whom shall we go? You have the words of eternal life. We have come to believe and are convinced that you are the Holy One of God." (John 6:67–69)

Peter and the rest of the Twelve would stay with Jesus, listening and learning.

We are born with desires for love, life, peace, beauty, and truth. We are hungry for all that, and our lives are a journey to find it. We are made by God, and it's for God that we hunger and thirst.

We don't know it all the time. We chase after all sorts of things to feed our hunger. We stand in front of that open refrigerator door and see some things that look good. They might fill us up for a while. But even the manna God sent from heaven did not satisfy the people's deepest hunger. All of us desire what only Jesus can give.

In the Eucharist, he shares his body and blood, his soul and divinity—his entire being—with you and me. When we go to Mass, we're present with the Apostles in the Upper Room at the Last Supper, and we're present at Jesus' sacrifice on the cross, all of it woven into the mystery that is exactly what Jesus said: his body and blood, his very life, given to us so that we'll never be hungry again.

To read the whole story in the Bible, go to Mark 6:34–42 and John chapter 6.

Think Quietly: What are the times in life when something has made you happy for a while but then lost its power to satisfy? What does Jesus promise?

Pray Together: Jesus, you are the bread of life. Thank you for sharing your life with us so that we can live forever with you.

Jesus said to them, "I am the bread of life."

"I Am the Good Shepherd"

In this noisy, busy world, who should we listen to?

The sheep hear his voice, as he calls his own sheep by name and leads them out. When he has driven out all his own, he walks ahead of them, and the sheep follow him, because they recognize his voice. (John 10:3–4)

When Jesus preached, he often used sheep and shepherds as examples. This wasn't just because his listeners were familiar with the care a good shepherd would give his sheep. They also were used to hearing God's work described as caring for his sheep. After all, one of the most familiar prayers in the Bible is

Psalm 23: "The LORD is my shepherd, I shall not want. . . ."

Jesus' listeners were used to the idea that people who led God's people were like shepherds. Moses and David had been described as shepherds. Five hundred years before Jesus came to earth, God spoke through Ezekiel to tell the people that he would come to earth to seek out the lost and scattered sheep of Israel. God would gather them back to him and feed them in fertile, lush pastures. Israel's leaders had failed. God himself would come to be their shepherd.

Jesus healed a man who had been blind from birth. He met the man, spat on the ground, mixed his saliva with dirt to make mud, and rubbed the mud on the man's eyes. He told the man to go wash. When the man washed the mud off his eyes, he could see for the first time in his life.

The Pharisees heard about what was going on, and so the man was brought to them. The religious leaders were confused because the man was healed on the Sabbath, when work was forbidden. This healer could not be from God. But the man could see. How else could this happen but through God's power? Who was this healer? they asked the man. All he could answer was that the healer must have been a prophet.

The man's parents swore that, yes, he had been blind from birth and, no, they didn't know anything about the healer. In the growing confusion, the man was brought back to the Pharisees, who tried to make him say that the healer must have been a sinner because he healed on the Sabbath.

The man couldn't say this. After all, he'd been healed, and that's God's work.

The Pharisees believed that the man was blind because of his own sin, but now the man could see. And Jesus had broken the law by healing on the Sabbath.

Nothing made sense to the Pharisees, and this made them angry.

So they threw the man out.

When Jesus heard that they had thrown him out, he found him and said, "Do you believe in the Son of Man?" He answered and said, "Who is he, sir, that I may believe in him?" Jesus said to him, "You have seen him and the one speaking with you is he." He said, "I do believe, Lord," and he worshiped him. (John 9:35–38)

And in Jesus' voice and in his words, the man experienced a different kind of healing. He could see now, not only with his eyes but with his whole being. Many voices had questioned him, had accused him of being blind because he was a sinner. These voices had told him that the one who healed him was a sinner, too. But when the voice of Jesus called out to him, he could finally understand who had given him the great gift of light and life.

Some of the Pharisees who had questioned the man were still around, and now they questioned Jesus. So Jesus started talking to them about sheep.

He described how sheep, kept in a pen, will come when their shepherd calls them, and they won't follow anyone else. They know the voice of the one who cares for and protects them. They trust him and will follow him. The Pharisees still couldn't see what this had to do with anything.

Jesus continued. He wasn't only the good shepherd; he was the gate, too. Others—false shepherds who don't love the sheep—come and try to steal the sheep or even kill them. Only if the sheep listen to him and follow him will they find good pasture and safety.

More than this, Jesus, like the best shepherds, is willing to die for his sheep. Everyone knew it was dangerous to be a shepherd. There were all kinds of wild animals that would kill and eat the sheep. And robbers could come and hurt the shepherd to steal his sheep. A hired hand would run away and leave the sheep unprotected. But the real shepherd, the one who loved the sheep, would stay and risk his life for them.

"I am the good shepherd. A good shepherd lays down his life for the sheep." (John 10:11)

> "A good shepherd lays down his life for the sheep."

The man born blind heard many voices. They questioned and challenged him. They told him that the one who had given him sight could not be from God. In fact, there must be something seriously wrong with the blind man and the one who healed him.

But in the voice of Jesus, the Good Shepherd, the man heard the truth, and so do we. Our Good Shepherd helps us see, and he reveals the truth about the world. He protects us and gives us life forever. We know his voice, and it's the voice of the one who knows us best and always leads us to safety.

To read the whole story, go to John chapters 9—10.

Think Quietly: What do the voices of this world try to tell you about what's important? What does Jesus tell us is important? What can Jesus give us that the world can't?

Pray Together: Jesus, you give sight to the blind. Help us see and live the truth always.

Jesus Calls Us to Live for Him

Every day, we have so many things to do. Some are fun, and some aren't. Some tasks are hard and others are boring. But they have to be done!

Everything we do—even the little, boring, or hard tasks—is part of a bigger picture, a picture of our family's life and our life at school. They're also part of an even bigger picture: why God put us on earth. It's a picture that's about love.

Jesus spoke a lot about the end of the world. He told parables about it and described what it would be like. When Jesus talks about the end of the world, we learn a lot about why God created the world. We learn why *we* were made and where *we're* going, right now. We learn about the big story that our life is part of.

Jesus told his friends that no one would know when the end of the world would come. He talked about being ready and awake, about paying attention and planning. And he talked about how the world will be judged. This is why: our lives are a gift from God. Every minute, every second is a gift. How are we using this gift? It matters.

One of the stories Jesus told was about sheep and goats.

Jesus said that, at the end of the world, the Son of Man would come with all the angels and sit on his throne—the throne was a symbol of judgment. All the world would be gathered before him, and he would separate them, just as a farmer separates sheep and goats.

> "I was hungry and you gave me food."

The sheep would be at the king's right hand, and the goats at his left. The people listening to Jesus would have known what that meant, because in their culture, to be at the king's right hand was a sign of blessing.

Jesus described what the king would say to the sheep. He would tell them that they would be with him forever because "I was hungry and you gave me food, I was thirsty and you gave me drink, a stranger and you welcomed me, naked and you clothed me, ill and you cared for me, in prison and you visited me." (Matthew 25:35–36)

That seemed so strange. Those at his right wondered when this had happened. They had never seen this king hungry or thirsty or in prison, had they?

But Jesus gave a simple answer. Whenever they had taken the small step of feeding someone who was hungry or giving drink to someone who was thirsty, or when they had welcomed a stranger, clothed the naked, cared for the sick, or visited the imprisoned—they had done all this for Jesus, the king.

And those on the king's left side? They, too, had met Jesus in people who needed help. But they had ignored those people. In little ways, they had turned their backs on Jesus' presence in others. And all those little ways added up. Their steps away from Jesus may have seemed small but were leading them far away.

God created each one of us. We're not here for random reasons or by accident. We're here because God wants us to be here—every single one of us. And each of us is created in God's image. God spoke and breathed each of us into being, out of love. When we know, accept, and live with this big story as our very own story, we can live with peace in our hearts. When we don't, we separate ourselves from all that God wants for us, from the story God has prepared for us.

Jesus brings us back to our place in God's great story. He brings us back by his Passion, Death, and Resurrection. He brings us back by staying with us on earth in his Body, the Church.

When life in the Body of Christ is the big story we live by, all those little steps of virtue and mercy make sense, no matter how hard they are to do. Those Corporal and Spiritual Works of Mercy become a way of life, and everything else fits.

We're friends of Jesus. We trace the sign of his cross on our bodies every day. We know that what he says is true: it's through following him that we find love, life, and peace that never end.

Jesus comes to us every day. He's the beginning and the end: the alpha and the omega. We have the gift of being able to meet and serve him every day in every person who comes our way. Letting the big story of God's love guide us in these moments, we're taking small steps with him and with the rest of the Body of

Christ to the place he promised: life with him forever. In that life, night will be no more, nor will they need light from lamp or sun, for the Lord God shall give them light, and they shall reign forever and ever. (Revelation 22:5)

To read the whole story in the Bible, go to Matthew 25:31–46 and Revelation chapter 22.

Think Quietly: How does keeping Jesus at the center of your life help guide your decisions? What's the final destination we're all hoping to reach?

Pray Together: Lord Jesus, you are the alpha and the omega, the beginning and the end. May I see you in every person I meet today.

Lent

The Garden of Eden

Genesis means "beginning." It's the first book of the Bible, and that's what it's about: beginnings.

It's about the beginnings of the world and everything in it: sun and moon, fish and flowers, and all sorts of creatures. Genesis is also the story of our beginnings—yours and mine. Genesis tells the beginning of the human story. Your story.

In the beginning, human beings were created by God, but he made them quite different from the other animals, not just on the outside but most importantly, on the inside.

We are made in God's image!

God created us to be free, creative, and loving. And in the beginning, we said yes to God—to the world he made and to all he had given us. Our first parents lived in the beauty God had given them.

Genesis also tells about another beginning. It tells the story of our saying no to God. And that "no" begins with temptation. It begins with a hint. A nudge.

Adam and Eve, our first parents, lived in the garden God had made for them. It was called the Garden of Eden. In that garden was everything they needed. They were free to eat the fruit of any tree in the garden except one: the tree of the knowledge of good and evil. God warned them that eating from this tree would lead to death.

A serpent came to Eve and pointed out that tree. Eve told the serpent what God had said. But this is what the serpent said: "You certainly will not die! God knows well that when you eat of it your eyes will be opened and you will be like gods, who know good and evil." (Genesis 3:4–5)

When the serpent said this, Eve looked at the tree again. Instead of thinking about God's warning, Eve thought about how delicious the fruit looked. She was tempted.

God had created Eve to be free. She could say yes to everything God had given her. She could say yes to trusting God. Or she could say no. She had a choice.

She chose to say no.

God welcomed people into the world of truth, beauty, and love he had created. When we say yes to God and trust God, we find peace. When we decide that we know better than God, we find trouble and sadness. That's exactly what the serpent wanted to happen to Eve and her husband, Adam.

After Eve tasted the fruit from the tree of the knowledge of good and evil, she gave some of the fruit to Adam, and he tried it, too. Then everything changed.

Before Adam and Eve disobeyed God's wishes, they had lived in the garden with each other, with nature, and with God, in perfect harmony, open and free, with nothing between them. But now they looked at each other, and they felt that something was very wrong.

Then, for the first time ever, Adam and Eve hid from the God who loved them.

When they heard the sound of the LORD God walking about in the garden at the breezy time of the day, the man and his wife hid themselves from the LORD God among the trees of the garden. The LORD God then called to the man and asked him: Where are you? He answered, "I heard you in the garden; but I was afraid, because I was naked, so I hid." Then God asked, "Who told you that you were naked? Have you eaten from the tree of which I had forbidden you to eat?" The man replied, "The woman whom you put here with me—she gave me fruit from the tree, so I ate it." The LORD God then asked the woman: What is this you have done? The woman answered, "The snake tricked me, so I ate it."
(Genesis 3:8–13)

The man admitted to God that they were hiding. They had no clothes on and felt ashamed for God to see them.

Well, they had *never* had clothes! The garden was a place of love and safety. They had trusted each other, and they had trusted God. So there was no need to cover up the beautiful bodies God had given them. What had changed? When they ate of the forbidden tree, they saw everything in a different way.

Of course, God already knew what had happened. They had eaten from the forbidden tree. The man blamed the woman, and the woman blamed the snake. As you can see, neither one of them admitted that they had made their own decision to say no to God.

In that choice to use their freedom to say no to God, Adam and Eve lost the beautiful garden paradise God had given them. By deciding they knew better than God, by saying no, the man and woman had put walls of separation between themselves and nature, between each other, and even between themselves and God.

⌐∽⌐

When we make choices that go against what is best for us, we suffer, don't we? God created us to love one another and to walk close beside him. But when we say no to that path, our lives get lost. We don't find the life God wants for us. It isn't easy to find our way back, is it?

If you have ever been lost, you know how terrible it feels. Why did you get lost in the first place? Maybe you were stubborn and didn't listen to directions. You might have been angry and just started walking away, thinking that you knew best and didn't need anyone's help.

Lent is a time to admit that we are lost. Our journey back can be challenging, because it is hard to admit our sins and mistakes. But it's a relief, too, because we don't have to be lost anymore. Our first parents picked the fruit of one tree that took us further away from God. Ahead, at Easter, we will see the wood of another tree, love waiting there, guiding us home.

To read the whole story in the Bible, go to Genesis chapter 3.

Think Quietly: When are you tempted to say no to God? What helps you say yes instead of no?

Pray Together: Creator God, you made us for love. Forgive us for the times we have said no to you.

> For the first time ever, Adam and Eve hid from the God who loved them.

The Brothers Cain and Abel

Now Adam and Eve lived outside the Garden of Eden. They worked hard on the land, and they began to have children. Their first two were sons. The older boy was Cain, and his younger brother was named Abel. Cain took care of crops out in the fields. Abel cared for sheep.

From very early in human life, even though people's understanding was darkened by sin and pride, they still understood that God had given them the world to live in, and they were grateful. They were thankful for their homes and for the food they had to eat. When we want to say thank you to someone, we know that words are not good enough. We want to *show* that we are grateful. And so, people long ago said thank you to God by giving something back to God. They offered God their best animals and their best crops. They sacrificed these things to say thank you.

Cain and Abel offered sacrifice, too. Cain was a farmer, so he brought grains to the altar for sacrifice. Abel was a shepherd, so he brought the best of the best, the firstborn lamb. When ancient people gave the first of their flocks, they were saying to God: I love you so much, I will give you the first of what I have. I trust that more will come, but even if it doesn't, you will care for me. Sacrifice was a sign of love and trust.

But when the two brothers offered their sacrifices, God favored Abel's sacrifice more than Cain's. We don't know why. That didn't mean that God loved Abel more than Cain. But when God was not as pleased with Cain's sacrifice, Cain became jealous of his brother. And his jealousy turned into anger.

> Cain became jealous of his brother.

Cain asked Abel to go into the field with him. Out there on the land God had given him, on the land where he grew food, Cain murdered his brother, Abel.

God called to Cain, "Where is your brother Abel?" He answered, "I do not know. Am I my brother's keeper?" (Genesis 4:9) That was his way of saying, "It's not my job to take care of my brother!"

God then said: "What have you done? Your brother's blood cries out to me from the ground!" (Genesis 4:10)

Because Cain had killed his brother, God said that the earth would no longer be fruitful for Cain. "If you till the ground, it shall no longer give you its produce. You shall become a constant wanderer on the earth." (Genesis 4:12) Adam and Eve's Original Sin had separated them from God, and now Cain would be separated even more as he wandered the earth. This made Cain afraid. He told God that he knew he would be killed by someone else now that he was completely on his own.

Even when we sin, God never leaves us. God told Cain that he would protect him, and he put a mark on Cain so that everyone would leave him alone. Then Cain wandered further away from his original home, many miles east of where the beautiful garden had been.

Every sin does harm to the world God made. Every time we choose to do something wrong, our hearts grow weaker in love. And our sin encourages others to sin, and so one sin can cause trouble for many people.

During Lent, we find a better way.

From the cross, Jesus forgave those who hurt him the worst, and during Lent, we step away from our own selfish path and follow Jesus to that path of love and forgiveness. We come to Jesus in the Sacrament of Reconciliation and confess the times we are selfish, jealous, and hurtful. We let Jesus fill us with peace.

During Lent, when we give up food or activities we like, we grow strong so that when the choice comes between selfishness and love, we'll be ready to choose love. We pray more so that we can learn to see people as God does and we can reach out in love to all people. And we try to be more helpful and give more to others, because that's the way Jesus lived, and we are his friends. We're friends of Jesus, who came to earth to teach us that, yes, we *are* our brother's keeper. We have one father, who loves us all.

To read the whole story in the Bible, go to Genesis 4:1–16.

Think Quietly: How has my sin affected other people?

Pray Together: Father, help us forgive others as you forgive us.

Abraham and His Son Isaac

Hundreds of years ago, God told a certain man to travel far from his homeland. The man didn't know what he would find in this new place. But he trusted God and followed him.

When the man began this journey, his name was Abram. The Book of Genesis tells us this story of Abram after we have learned about how God created a good, beautiful world and human beings to live in it. Abram's story comes to us after we have learned about how human beings misused the gift of free will to say no to God. And the world became so evil that God had to bring a great flood and then start all over again.

When we meet Abram, the new world is filled with people again. They have begun to create cities. Abram lived in a place called Ur, in a part of the world that is now Iraq, where some of the world's earliest civilizations began.

In Abram's time, people lived in large families. You didn't just live with your mother and father and brothers and sisters. You created a big camp with all your aunts and uncles and cousins and grandparents. Abram's family were nomads. They raised animals such as sheep and goats, and they traveled all over the country, wherever their animals could find grass to eat. Abram had a wife named Sarai, but they had no children.

God led Abram from Ur, then to Haran, which is in the land we now call Turkey, then all the way to Canaan, the Promised Land, which we now call Israel. And there, in Canaan, God made a covenant with Abram. In this solemn agreement, God promised Abram that he would have descendants as numerous as the stars in the sky. God was choosing Abram's family to bring light back into the world.

That was God's side of the covenant: to protect and guide Abram and all his descendants. Abram's family would have a part, too. As a sign of his new relationship to God, his name would be changed to Abraham, and his wife's name would change to Sarah. Through Abraham's family, the world would learn that there is only one God, the God of all people, everywhere, and of the whole universe. This God created every person and wanted to draw all people back to himself in love.

Even though Abraham and Sarah were old, God did keep his promise and gave them a son, and they named him Isaac. They had a good life! They lived in the Promised Land. And they now had a son who would someday have sons and daughters of his own. Just as

God said, Abraham's descendants would be as numerous as the stars in the sky or the sand on the beach.

Then one day, God called to Abraham. Abraham answered right away, "Here I am!"

Then God said, "Take your son Isaac, your only one, whom you love, and go to the land of Moriah. There offer him up as a burnt offering on one of the heights that I will point out to you." (Genesis 22:2)

And so Abraham, who was faithful to God, obeyed. The next morning, Abraham cut wood to take so that they could make the fire. He called two servants to travel with them. Then he and Isaac and the two servants began their journey to Moriah. We do not know what Abraham was thinking that morning as he set out for the place God directed him to. We do not know what he was thinking on that third day when, at a distance, he saw the mountains of the land of Moriah, and he knew what God was asking him to do there.

All we know is that he obeyed God, told the servants to wait, put the wood on Isaac's back, carried the fire and the knife, and walked up the mountain with his son.

As the two walked on together, Isaac spoke to his father Abraham: "Father!" he said. "Here I am," he replied. Isaac continued, "Here are the fire and the wood, but where is the sheep for the burnt offering?" "My son," Abraham answered, "God will provide the sheep for the burnt offering." Then the two walked on together. (Genesis 22:6–8)

After a three-day journey, Abraham and Isaac reached the place God had shown Abraham. He built an altar. He laid down the wood, and finally, he tied up Isaac, his only son, and laid him on the altar, on top of the wood. Abraham took out the knife to kill his son, when an angel of God called out from heaven.

"Abraham, Abraham!" "Here I am," he answered. "Do not lay your hand on the boy," said the angel. "Do not do the least thing to him. For now I know that you fear God, since you did not withhold from me your son, your only one." (Genesis 22:11–12)

Then Abraham saw that a ram was caught in a bush nearby. This was the sacrifice God had provided.

~~~

> God said, "Take your son Isaac, your only one, whom you love."

We listen to this story from Abraham's life and reflect on it every year during Lent. The earliest followers of Jesus read the story of Abraham and Isaac, and it reminded them of Jesus, God's only Son, and his journey to the cross. It helped them understand how faithful God is to his people. It helped them understand that Jesus is the Lamb of God, who gave himself in sacrifice for our sins.

For us today, the season of Lent is a journey like Abraham's. God calls us to follow him and go where he leads. We are not sure what lies ahead, but we trust God to lead us. We're not alone, either. Our Lenten path is a journey of sacrifice with all of God's people, who are as numerous as the stars in the sky.

To read the whole story in the Bible, go to Genesis 22:1–19.

Think Quietly: What sacrifices are you making during Lent? How can you help others on their Lenten journey?

Pray Together: God of Abraham, be with us on our journey. We trust in you.

Moses Leads God's People

God's people were on a long journey. It began in Egypt, where the people had been slaves for four hundred years. God chose Moses to help lead the people out of slavery and away from Egypt to the land God had given them long ago through Abraham: their home.

This journey would take forty years. God's people spent forty years in the desert, and during that time, they learned how to walk with God. They walked and listened. They made mistakes, and sometimes they said no to God and walked away from him. But then God showed them how to walk beside him again. The

Israelites' long time in the desert was a journey of faith.

The people's journey in the wilderness was hard, and sometimes they were afraid. But they were not alone. God showed them the way, in the form of a cloud during the day and a pillar of fire by night.

There weren't any grocery stores or farms on the way. The people worried about this and complained to God. God fed them by giving them a miraculous food called manna, which appeared on the ground every morning like the dewfall.

The people complained about being thirsty, too. They asked Moses why God had led them out of Egypt if he was going to let them die from thirst in the desert—what good was that?

Moses became frustrated because the people complained so much. He prayed to God, "What shall I do with these people?" God told Moses to take his staff and use it to hit a rock. Water would come out of the rock. Moses followed God's instructions, and water came out of the rock, and the people could drink all they needed.

Out in the wilderness, God came to his people and gave them a great gift, greater than directions for their journey or food and water. God gave them a way of life that would be a light in the world's darkness.

It happened on a mountain called Sinai, a great mountain on a triangle of land between Egypt and the Promised Land.

Three months after they left Egypt, the people reached the mountain, and God told Moses to prepare the people, to tell them to make themselves ready and pure for God's coming. He said to remind them of what he had done for them, how he had brought them out of slavery into freedom. It was time for them to renew the

> Moses became frustrated because the people complained so much.

covenant God had made with Abraham long ago. These were his Chosen People, called out of slavery, not just for their own sake, but to be a blessing for the entire world.

Now, if you obey me completely and keep my covenant, you will be my treasured possession among all peoples. (Exodus 19:5)

Ever since our first parents had said no to God, God had been reaching back into his creation and inviting us back to him. The way of life God was going to give Israel would help the world see how to say yes again.

And so, the people prepared. They cleaned themselves and prayed. They watched as Moses went up the mountain, but they were careful not to get too close. They knew that God would be present on the mountain, and that God's holiness was too powerful for them to bear.

Thunder roared and lightning flashed. The people heard what sounded like trumpets. Smoke surrounded the mountain, fires flared, and the mountain shook. Moses was on the mountain, and he was in the presence of God.

When Moses came back down the mountain, he had good news to share with the people of Israel. God had given them instructions for living that would help them be their best. This way of life would create peace, truth, and justice for the poor. It was called the Law.

The core of the Law is the Ten Commandments, and God had given the Ten Commandments to Moses on tablets of stone. It began:

I am the LORD your God, who brought you out of the land of Egypt, out of the house of slavery. You shall not have other gods beside me. (Exodus 20:2–3)

The Law continued, going into great detail about how the people should worship, how they should take care of the bodies God had created, and how they should treat one another. Over the centuries, the Jewish people have studied this Law, explained it, and even argued about how to live by it. It has always been for them what God intended: a way for them to live that reflects God's goodness, truth, mercy, and care.

Israel spent forty years learning from God in the desert. They suffered and sacrificed. They learned new things about God. They listened to God's Word. They sinned and were unfaithful to God at times, but he forgave them. They stayed on the journey.

In the Bible, we learn about this journey in the books of Exodus, Leviticus, Numbers, and Deuteronomy. We read about the journey during the season of Lent. On our Lenten journey of forty days, we, too, are in a kind of wilderness. We've given up food and activities that gave us comfort and happiness, but we're trusting that God will fill our emptiness. We're listening more closely to God. We're praying and worshipping God, and he feeds us and gives us another kind of manna: himself in the Eucharist. We confess our sins and receive God's mercy. We're God's people, and we're on a journey, learning to walk with God more closely.

To read the whole story in the Bible, go to Exodus 17:3–7 and 20:1–17.

Think Quietly: What did God give Israel during the forty years in the desert? How does God take care of you on the journey of your life?

Pray Together: Lord, be our protector and guide on our journey, now and always.

The Devil Tempts Jesus in the Desert

For forty days, Jesus had lived in the desert. He had walked in this hilly, rocky place full of caves and scrubby plants. He had fasted all that time—no food for forty days. He had prayed. Jesus was getting ready to go out into the world and begin his ministry. First, he needed to spend time alone with his heavenly Father, praying and listening.

But now, Jesus was no longer alone. He had a visitor, and the visitor had something to say.

"Do you see those stones?" The visitor pointed to the ground, knowing that after weeks of fasting, Jesus was extremely hungry. "You are God's Son. You could just turn those stones into bread and eat them." Jesus recognized this visitor. It was the Devil. And the Devil pressured Jesus to use his power to satisfy himself.

Jesus' many days alone in the desert, spending time with his heavenly Father, had helped prepare him for the Devil's tricks. Jesus had an answer for this temptation, and it was straight from God's Word:

> "One does not live by bread alone,
> but by every word that comes forth
> from the mouth of God." (Matthew 4:4)

Jesus recognized this visitor. It was the Devil.

The Devil decided to tempt Jesus with something important to Jesus and all other Jewish people: the temple in Jerusalem. The temple was the center of worship for God's people. It was there they offered sacrifice in gratitude to God. It was there they kept the tablets with the Law that Moses had brought down from Mount Sinai. Jesus had visited this temple with his family to pray and give thanks and offer sacrifice.

So the Devil took Jesus to the very highest point of this temple and challenged him. "If you are really the Son of God," he said, "throw yourself down from here and have the angels come rescue you."

Again, Jesus answered from God's Word: "You shall not put the Lord, your God, to the test." (Matthew 4:7)

Finally, the Devil showed Jesus the whole world. "Worship me" he said, "and all of this will be yours."

Jesus spoke a command God had given his people a long time ago:

> "The Lord, your God, shall you worship
> and him alone shall you serve." (Matthew 4:10)

And with that, the Devil left, and angels came to Jesus to help him. He had passed a difficult test, but now he was ready to begin teaching others about God.

We are friends of Jesus. He walks with us, and we walk with him everywhere—even into the desert. Every day, the Devil tries to tempt us, too. We are tempted to push God away. We are tempted to use good things in this world—such as food or money—just for ourselves.

During our own forty days in the desert of Lent, we fast, too. We give up certain foods and other treats or fun activities that are important to us. We take time we might spend playing and pray a little bit more instead. We get to know people who need help, and we help them through our time or our money or other gifts. We let go of things that seem important and give them to God. When we do this, we often learn that we don't need those things as much as we thought.

We sometimes think that doing without will make us weaker, but we find that, in the desert with Jesus, we're stronger. We find out that God gives us everything we need, and we want to share those gifts with others. We are Jesus' friends, and we are with him in the desert, depending on God's Word. We are there saying no to darkness and selfishness, and saying yes to God's love.

To read the whole story in the Bible, go to Matthew 4:1–11 and Luke 4:1–13.

Think Quietly: What am I giving up during Lent? What temptations are hard for me to resist? Why is it important for me to keep trying?

Pray Together: Jesus, we are with you in the desert. We are being tempted, but we know that you will help us stay strong. We pray that our time in the desert with you will help us love you and all people more.

Jesus Heals a Man Who Is Paralyzed

We'll do a lot to help our friends, won't we? We help them when they ask for it—or even when they are afraid to ask. We stick up for them when other people treat them badly. And most of all, we spend time with our friends, and we listen to them. We'd do anything for our friends.

Would you lower your friend down through a roof into a big crowd of people? Maybe if Jesus was in the middle of that room, you would!

This is what some friends did for a man who was very sick. He was paralyzed, and he couldn't walk at all. His friends heard about Jesus and wondered if he could help their friend.

They heard that Jesus was teaching people in the home of Peter, one of the fishermen who had decided to follow Jesus and learn from him. So they found Peter's house, and it was true—the place was full of people, because Jesus was inside teaching. You couldn't even get through a door or window.

In those days, houses had walls made of mud bricks and wood. The roofs were flat, made with wood frames that were covered in grass, sticks, and dirt. The friends carried the paralyzed man on a mat. They were sure Jesus could help their friend. But there were so many people in the house, and the doors were so narrow, there was no space for them. So up to the roof they climbed.

> "I say to you, rise, pick up your mat, and go home."

Unable to get near Jesus because of the crowd, they opened up the roof above him. After they had broken through, they let down the mat on which the paralytic was lying. (Mark 2:4)

You can imagine the surprise of the crowd listening to Jesus when the dust and grass started falling around them! And then, there was a man on a mat being lowered down right in the middle of the room.

When Jesus saw this, he admired the faith of this man's friends. And he said to the paralyzed man, "Your sins are forgiven."

What a strange thing to say! Jesus, a man, had told another man that his sins were forgiven. Only God could forgive sins! Who did this Jesus think he was?

Jesus knew what people were thinking, so he explained. But he also acted. He asked them which was easier to say to the paralyzed person: "Your sins are forgiven" or "Pick up your mat and walk"?

"But that you may know that the Son of Man has authority to forgive sins on earth"—he said to the paralytic, "I say to you, rise, pick up your mat, and go home." (Mark 2:10–11)

The man did just that—he stood up and picked up the mat he'd been lying on.

Everyone was amazed. They began to understand that Jesus was more than just a man. God had given him the ability to heal a paralyzed man. Maybe God could speak through Jesus and forgive the man's sins, too.

The paralyzed man had a serious problem with his body. His friends believed that Jesus could fix this problem. That's why they went to all that trouble to bring him to Jesus. They probably thought that their friend's biggest problem was not being able to walk.

So why didn't Jesus help him with that first? Why did he forgive the man's sins before he did anything else? The friends and the sick man probably weren't even thinking about his sins. They probably weren't thinking about the ways he was separated from God or had hurt others.

But Jesus knew. And Jesus knew that no matter what else was going on in the man's life, his relationship with God was the most important thing. Even if he walked again, if he was still far from God and not listening to God, his life would never be at peace, and he wouldn't be truly happy.

Our bodies may be strong, or our bodies may be weak. But if our souls are paralyzed with sin, we can't love God or others.

During these days of Lent, we—like the people in this story—are trying to get closer to Jesus. We may have to put away things that distract us so we can listen more carefully. We may have to give up activities we enjoy so that we can learn how Jesus gives true happiness.

We will take a few more minutes every day to try to listen to Jesus in prayer. We will be like the friends in this story and try to bring others to Jesus.

And we might come up close to Jesus in the Sacrament of Reconciliation. We know that any sin can paralyze our hearts and minds because it keeps us from living in a way that is free and loving. When we confess our sins, we can start moving again. We can love more and help more. We can pick up our mats and walk—maybe even run—to Jesus' loving arms.

For the whole story in the Bible, go to Mark 2:1–12.

Think Quietly: In what ways does my life need Jesus' healing touch?

Pray Together: Jesus, we come to you, trusting that you can heal us. We are helping each other find you this Lent. Forgive us our sins, and help us walk again.

The Story of Two Sons

People were hearing more and more about this man Jesus who was preaching and teaching in towns and out in the countryside. They heard that he was a wise teacher. He also healed those who were sick. He even forgave sins! But there was something else about Jesus that people talked about. Jesus was known for the company he kept. Which was *anybody* and *everybody* who wanted to see him.

Back then, people believed that it was best to stay away from people who were known for being sinners. They believed that if you spent time with others who did not obey God's Law, you would not be worthy to be in God's presence, either.

People were confused and worried when they saw Jesus talking to sinners and even going to their homes for dinner. Wasn't he doing something wrong? Jesus tried to help them understand by telling stories. One of the stories he told was about a man who had two sons.

The sons grew up, and the younger son decided he wanted to be on his own. He asked his father if he could have his share of the family money now instead of after his father died. The father agreed and gave the son his portion of the money. The son moved far away from his home and his family.

At first, everything went fine. The younger son used his money to enjoy himself in that distant land. But he didn't pay much attention to how fast he was spending his money. He didn't make plans for the future—he just had a good time with his friends. You can guess what happened. He ran out of money—he spent it all! And he didn't have any way to earn more. And the friends who enjoyed his parties stopped coming around when they found out he was out of money. He had to work for a farmer, taking care of the pigs. He was so hungry that he felt like eating the scraps he was feeding the animals.

He had left home thinking that if he could just do what he wanted, he would be free. He would enjoy his life. But he had done what he wanted, and now he wasn't free at all. He was working like a slave—and he was still hungry

Then the young man realized something. The servants who worked for his father were much better off than he was now. They had plenty of food and a warm place to sleep. He needed to go back home.

This would not be easy. The son knew that he could not just walk into his father's house as if nothing had happened. So he thought, I shall get up and go to my father and I shall say to him, "Father, I have sinned against heaven and against you. I no longer deserve to be called your son; treat me as you would treat one of your hired workers." (Luke 15:18–20)

So the son set out on his way. He walked and walked. It was a long journey back to his father.

How surprised the young man was when, before he had even reached the house, there was his father, running out to meet him. His arms were open. He wasn't angry. He didn't scold. He ran up to his long-lost son, and hugged and kissed him. The father was overjoyed.

The son tried to talk. "Father, I have sinned against heaven and against you; I no longer deserve to be called your son." But his father ordered his servants. "Quickly bring the finest robe and put it on him; put a ring on his finger and sandals on his feet. Take the fattened calf and slaughter it. Then let us celebrate with a feast, because this son of mine was dead, and has come to life again; he was lost, and has been found." Then the celebrations began. (Luke 15:21–24)

But don't forget—there was someone else at home, too. The older brother had never left. He had worked hard and obeyed his father all along. And he hadn't spent his inheritance—his money was still safe. But as he watched this celebration and saw his father's joy, this older son became angry and jealous.

After all, he had been good the whole time. It was his little brother who had run away and sinned and lost everything. He said to his father, "Look, all these years I served you and not once did I disobey your orders; yet you never gave me even a young goat to feast on with my friends." (Luke 15:29)

The loving father reassured his older son. "My son, you are here with me always; everything I have is yours. But now we must celebrate and rejoice, because your brother was dead and has come to life again; he was lost and has been found." (Luke 15:31–32)

We can see ourselves in this story, can't we? Sometimes we feel like the younger son who gets into trouble and has to come home. Sometimes we feel like the older brother who stays out of trouble but doesn't love others very well. And sometimes we feel like the father, when someone has hurt us but asks us to forgive them.

God is our Father, and with him, every day is a chance to say we are sorry for the times we have done the wrong thing. Or we can admit that we've done the right thing but with a bad attitude. Notice how the father doesn't even wait for the son to come all the way home. He runs out to meet him! He loves his son that much!

> "I no longer deserve to be called your son."

Every day, God waits for us. During Lent, we have a chance to think more carefully about our lives. How have we wandered away from God? How have we wasted what God has given us? And when have we been jealous because God showed mercy to someone else? We have a chance to come close to him and admit what we have done. We can tell God how much we want to change. Through this story about the two sons, Jesus shows us that even when we sin, God loves us and wants us close to him, not far away. We're on our way back to God, and God is waiting with open arms.

For the whole story, go to Luke 15:11–32.

Think Quietly: What gifts has God the Father given me? Have I used those gifts in good ways? Have I wasted them?

Pray Together: God, you are our loving Father. Thank you for your merciful love.

A Samaritan Woman Meets Jesus at the Well

In the middle of a hot, dry day, a woman was doing what she did every day: getting water from a well. She would fill her jars with water to cook with and clean with, and water to drink when she was thirsty. Every day, the woman needed water to live, and every day, she walked to the well to get it.

This day, though, there was something different about the well—Jacob's Well, they called it, after their father in faith who had dug it hundreds of years before. Today, a strange man was sitting nearby. He was alone. It looked as if he had been on a journey and now he was resting.

She didn't know it, but the man's name was Jesus. He said to her, "Give me a drink."

This was shocking. Men did not speak to women out in public, unless they were in the same family. There was another reason the woman did not expect Jesus to talk to her.

The Samaritan woman said to him, "How can you, a Jew, ask me, a Samaritan woman, for a drink?" (For Jews use nothing in common with Samaritans.) (John 4:9)

Jews and Samaritans believed that **Abraham** and Jacob and Moses were the fathers of their faith. But they worshipped in different places: the Samaritans in Shechem and the Jews in Jerusalem.

Jesus answered . . . , "If you knew the gift of God and who is saying to you, 'Give me a drink,' you would have asked him and he would have given you living water." (John 4:10)

The woman was talking about water that helps our bodies. But Jesus talked about a different kind of thirst and a different kind of water. Jesus was leading her to think about her life more deeply. She didn't understand, though, and just asked him how he could give her this water—he didn't even have a bucket with him!

> "Whoever drinks the water I shall give will never thirst."

"Everyone who drinks this water will be thirsty again; but whoever drinks the water I shall give will never thirst; the water I shall give will become in him a spring of water welling up to eternal life." The woman said to him, "Sir, give me this water, so that I may not be thirsty or have to keep coming here to draw water." (John 4:13–15)

Doesn't that sound wonderful? Have you ever been totally thirsty? Then you know how great it feels to finally quench that thirst. But even with that great feeling, you know it won't last. You'll get thirsty again.

We are hungry and thirsty for a lot of things. We thirst for love, truth, beauty, and life most of all. Our thirst is satisfied in many ways, and we do these things over and over again, but we all learn that they satisfy us for only a short time.

Jesus knows this. He knows how thirsty we are, and what we are trying to find. We are thirsty for what truly satisfies us as human beings: love, life, and truth.

Then Jesus told the woman to go get her husband. The woman answered, "I do not have a husband." Jesus answered her, "You are right in saying, 'I do not have a husband.' For you have had five husbands, and the one you have now is not your husband." (John 4:17–18)

Think of what Jesus was telling this woman. He knew that she was doing the same thing over and over again—getting married—because there was deep thirst in her life for love. Jesus knew all about her, what she had been doing to try to feel happy. He also knew what could help her.

Jesus could see right into the woman's heart, and she knew he must be a prophet. She and Jesus talked about this. They talked about a time in the future when the place we worship won't matter, because we'll all be worshipping God in spirit and truth.

The woman knew about that future time: it would be when the Messiah came. Jesus had news for her: "I am he, the one who is speaking to you."

Jesus knows *us*. He knows everything about us, even what we don't want anyone to know. He talks to us just as he talked to the Samaritan woman. He tells us who we really are, and we learn who *he* really is. Like that woman, we are so happy to find this living water that we have to go share the Good News!

Many of the Samaritans of that town began to believe in him because of the word of the woman who testified, "He told me everything I have done." When the Samaritans came to him, they invited him to stay with them; and he stayed there two days. Many more began to believe in him because of his word. (John 4:39–41)

In the waters of our Baptism, Jesus brings us to him. We can turn to him because he knows everything about us. He knows what we are thirsty for. And he has the love that will satisfy us now and always.

Right now, during Lent, many people around the world are getting ready to be baptized at Easter. There is a well full of living water waiting for them. Whoever they are, Jesus is waiting, welcoming them, meeting them, and giving them—and all of us—the living water of his truth, life, mercy, and love.

We'll never be thirsty again!

For the whole story in the Bible, go to John 4:1–42.

Think Quietly: What are your deepest wants? What will satisfy them? What can Jesus give you that none of these things can?

Pray Together: Jesus, you meet us at the well. We drink the living water you offer, and we are grateful.

Jesus Cleans Out the Temple

In the universe, on the earth, in the Promised Land, in the city called Jerusalem, a temple stood.

Here, God's people came to worship. Long ago, King David's son Solomon built this temple. It was glorious, shining, and beautiful because God is so great and we want to offer him the best. In the temple, God's people kept the Ark of the Covenant, which held the tablets of the Law that God had given Moses.

But as the years went by, Israel was invaded and conquered several times. The people were taken away from the land God had given them. The temple was destroyed, and the Ark of the Covenant was lost. Later, when the people returned to their land, they worked on rebuilding the temple.

Jewish people who did not live in Jerusalem prayed from the Scriptures and learned about God wherever they happened to live. But sacrifices could be offered only at the temple in Jerusalem. Priests offered to God the birds, goats, sheep, and other animals that people brought to express their thanks to God. These sacrifices were also a way the people could say they were sorry for their sins.

In the very center of the temple was the small space where the sacrifices were offered. Only the priests—such as John the Baptist's father—could enter there. Right outside that Holy of Holies were courts where the Jewish people who were not priests could gather to be near the sacrifice. And outside of that was another court, which was big and busy because anyone could go there. It was called the Court of the Gentiles. Gentiles were people who were not Jewish. Only Jewish people could participate in the sacrifices. But from the beginning, the prophets had reminded the Jewish people that the story of the world would end with all people, from every nation, gathering in peace and harmony on God's holy mountain. God's love was for everyone.

One day, the temple was quite busy. People from Jerusalem and other places were walking around, praying, and getting ready to worship. Then, suddenly, a man entered the crowd, shouting. Tables tumbled over, animals escaped from their pens, and money clanked on the ground. What could be happening?

> "Stop making my Father's house a marketplace."

Jesus was that man. He was angry. He found in the temple area those who sold oxen, sheep, and doves, as well as the money-changers seated there. He made a whip out of cords and drove them all out of the temple area, with the sheep and oxen, and spilled the coins of the money-changers and overturned their tables, and to those who sold doves he said, "Take these out of here, and stop making my Father's house a marketplace." (John 2:14–16)

This outer court was supposed to be a place where people of any nation could come and hear the Word of God. But it had become a market. People who did not have their own animals to bring for sacrifice could buy them there. Also, because money that came from other countries was not allowed in the temple, there were money changers, who exchanged foreign money—and of course, they charged fees for this.

Jesus said harsh words that day. He was angry because, in a place where people should be focused on God, they were focusing on how they could profit. His actions were forceful and strong, just like those of the prophets of the Old Testament who had pointed out sin and called people to return to the Lord.

Jesus said something else that day, which people remembered and repeated later, when Jesus was put on trial. Jesus looked around and said, "Destroy this temple, and in three days I will raise it up." (John 2:19)

This temple, which was the place where the people believed God came closest to them, had been destroyed and rebuilt. All the people knew this, and they knew it had taken many years to do it. Yet Jesus said he could do it in three days!

He was speaking about the temple of his body. Therefore, when he was raised from the dead, his disciples remembered that he had said this, and they came to believe the scripture and the word Jesus had spoken. (John 2:19–22)

The temple was a holy place where people could meet God. But it stood in only one spot on the earth. It was built by people, and it would be destroyed by people.

In Jesus, we have a new temple. In his body, God reaches down to us, touches us, and pulls us close to him, no matter where we live. Jesus gave his body as a sacrifice for our sins—this sacrifice would end all other sacrifices. The Church, which reaches to every corner of the earth, is that body, and we share in Jesus' sacrifice every time we go to Mass.

During Lent, we gather with people all over the world to worship God in this new temple without walls—this Body of Christ. But does Jesus need to enter our lives and clean them up, as he did in the temple that day? St. Paul tells us that our bodies are temples of the Holy Spirit. During Lent, we invite Jesus to cleanse those temples as we give up certain food and other activities.

We also listen to his challenge to the money changers, and we remember that whenever Jesus speaks in the Gospels, he is speaking to us, too. We listen humbly, and we think about why we go to Mass and how we spend our time there. We pay special attention to our attitudes toward prayer and worship, making sure we are focused on God in humility, gratitude, and love.

For the whole story in the Bible, go to John 2:13–25.

Think Quietly: What was going on in the temple that made Jesus angry? What did Jesus say about himself and the temple? In what ways do I need the temple that God has given me cleansed?

Pray Together: Jesus, we are sorry for being self-centered in prayer. Help deepen our reverence in worship and prayer time.

Nicodemus Brings Questions to Jesus

So many people were coming to see Jesus now.

They came to hear his stories and his wise teaching. They came because they heard that he could heal their broken bodies and make their sick children well. They heard that Jesus taught with God's authority—he could even forgive sins. So they gathered in towns and on hillsides. They crowded into homes and around the lake. Wherever Jesus was, they found him.

Nicodemus was interested in what Jesus had to say, but he couldn't come with the crowds, in public. Nicodemus had to come in secret because he was a

Pharisee. The Pharisees believed that the Law was a gift from God and that the people could live holy lives only because they followed every detail of the Law. These details told them what they could or could not eat, when they must rest, and what kinds of activities they should stay away from.

But Jesus came to God's people with good news. He didn't say that God's Law was not good or important. The Law taught the people how to honor God and how to be fair and kind. But Jesus knew that a person could follow all the rules of the Law and still have a heart that did not honor God, that was not fair or kind. Through faith in Jesus as God's Chosen One, the people could experience deep change in their hearts. The Law pointed people toward holiness, but Jesus helped them *become* holy, inside and out.

The Pharisees and scribes (teachers of the Law) were so concerned about following God's Law that they had created all kinds of rules to help people follow it better. The Law said that people should not work on the Sabbath, so the scribes and Pharisees said it was wrong even to pick grain to eat on the Sabbath. Jesus and his disciples did things like pick grain on the Sabbath because Jesus understood that God gave laws to the people to make life better, not harder. The teachers of the Law made it seem that God was far away unless people did everything perfectly. But Jesus said that God's kingdom was already here, right among the people.

You can imagine that Jesus' words and actions made the Pharisees nervous, even angry sometimes. *They* were the teachers of God's Law—and here was this man teaching something different! Who was he, and what did he think he was doing? In the Gospel stories, we often see the scribes and Pharisees at the edges of the crowd, trying to listen to Jesus and figure him out. Sometimes they asked him questions, and sometimes they scolded him for not obeying every rule they had written.

Nicodemus, who was a Pharisee, loved God's people and God's Law. And he had an open heart that wanted to learn. He wanted to hear more of what Jesus had to say. But he knew that the other Pharisees would be upset with him if they found out. So during the night, he searched for Jesus, and finally, he found him.

Nicodemus had heard of the miracles that Jesus performed. He mentioned this right away. He said that, because of these signs, it was clear that Jesus had come from God.

Jesus said, "I say to you, no one can see the kingdom of God without being born from above." (John 3:3)

Nicodemus was confused at first. He thought Jesus was talking about being born like a baby. He asked Jesus how this could be, because no one can return to their mother's womb and be born again into the world.

But Jesus wasn't talking about that kind of birth. He was talking about the life of a child of God—a spiritual birth.

"No one can enter the kingdom of God without being born of water and Spirit. What is born of flesh is flesh and what is born of spirit is spirit." (John 3:5–6)

They continued to talk. Nicodemus understood that the Law was a gift from God. But now Jesus told him that there was an even greater gift standing right there, talking with him. Jesus said,

For God so loved the world that he gave his only Son, so that everyone who believes in him might not perish but might have eternal life. (John 3:16)

<hr/>

We are all born into the world. But the life Jesus talks about is eternal—it takes us beyond this world. Jesus is here with us, and he leads us into that life with him. He changes our hearts and minds so that we can love God and follow his ways. That is the other way of being born in the Spirit. Jesus is here to help us. *God loves us that much.*

Most of us have been reborn in water and the spirit through our Baptisms. Jesus is part of our lives, and every day we share in his grace.

During Lent, we think about how Nicodemus went to Jesus during the night. Are we afraid, sometimes, to meet Jesus in our everyday life, where it's light and people can see us? During Lent, we stop being so busy with life in the world, and we take more time to be quiet and pray. In that prayer, in the light of God's love, we hear Jesus more clearly. He is speaking words that might confuse us at first, that might challenge us. But we have been reborn in the Spirit, so we can hear him now and we can understand: *For God so loved the world.*

> "For God so loved the world that he gave his only Son."

For the whole story in the Bible, go to John 3:1–21.

Think Quietly: How does Baptism change a person's life? How does your Baptism help you every day?

Pray Together: Jesus, in you we are born again in water and the Spirit. Lead us to eternal life with you.

The Transfiguration of Jesus

The word had spread about Jesus. People were coming from near and far to see him.

But who was this man? This was a hard question to answer. God's people knew about Abraham and Moses, about prophets such as Isaiah and Ezekiel. Jesus seemed to be like these prophets and teachers. But he spoke with even more authority than they had. He healed people's bodies, but he also healed their spirits when he forgave their sins.

One day, Jesus asked his friends what people were saying about him. They said that some people thought he was like John the Baptist or Elijah or one of the prophets. But when Jesus asked the disciples this same question, "Who do you say that I am?" Peter said, "You are the Messiah, the Son of the living God." (Matthew 16:16)

At that moment, Jesus also told Peter that he was the "rock" (that's what *Peter* means) and that the Church would be built on him. This is why we call Peter the first pope, the leader of the Church on earth.

From that time on, Jesus began to show his disciples that he must go to Jerusalem and suffer greatly from the elders, the chief priests, and the scribes, and be killed and on the third day be raised. Then Peter took him aside and began to rebuke him, "God forbid, Lord! No such thing shall ever happen to you." (Matthew 16:21–22)

Jesus responded to Peter by saying that Peter was putting his own ideas above God's will. Then he warned all the disciples about the trouble that would come. If they stayed with him, they would suffer too.

"If anyone wishes to come after me, he must deny himself and take up his cross daily and follow me. For whoever wishes to save his life will lose it, but whoever loses his life for my sake will save it." (Luke 9:23–24)

Following Jesus was not going to be easy! Such hard words might discourage some people, but not Jesus' friends. About a week later, we see that they are still on the journey with him. Jesus took Peter, James, and John with him up a mountain, where he began to pray.

In the long story of God's people, they often met God on mountaintops. Moses met God and received the Law on Mount Sinai. God passed by the prophet Ezekiel as a soft, quiet breeze when Ezekiel was in a cave on a mountainside. Jesus taught on hilltops, he went to a mountain to pray, and he was crucified on a hill called Golgotha. Before

Jesus, Moses, and Elijah talked about what Jesus was going to do in Jerusalem.

he ascended into heaven, he gathered his friends on a mountain before sending them out into the whole world to share the Good News.

Now, as Jesus was praying, Peter and John saw something amazing happen. Jesus seemed to be filled with light. His clothes became whiter than any person could make them. Most amazing of all, Moses and the prophet Elijah appeared right there in front of them.

Jesus, Moses, and Elijah talked about what Jesus was going to do in Jerusalem. Peter was frightened but also full of wonder. He wanted to make this mysterious event last longer. He said, "Lord, it is good that we are here. If you wish, I will make three tents here, one for you, one for Moses, and one for Elijah." (Matthew 17:4)

But then a cloud made a shadow over them, and out of the cloud a voice said, "This is my beloved Son, with whom I am well pleased; listen to him." (Matthew 17:5)

When the cloud disappeared and the friends could see clearly again, Moses and Elijah were gone. Only Jesus was there with them. And now it was time to go down from the mountain and get back on their way to Jerusalem.

Jesus' friends knew now that he was the Messiah, but they did not quite understand what that meant. Jesus was telling them that his way was a way of the Cross and a way of suffering. But he was also sharing with them the very good news that suffering would not be the end of the story, and that they should not be afraid.

The disciples saw Jesus in his glory on the mountain. This gave them courage to face whatever would happen in Jerusalem. In the same way, our Baptism gives us strength and courage. Every time we receive Jesus in the Eucharist, we meet him just as closely as the Apostles did on the mountain. He comes to us, and when he does, we can say to him, in gratitude and wonder, just like Peter, *Lord, it is good for us to be here!*

To read more about this event, go to Matthew 16:13—17:13; Mark 8:27–38; 9:2–9; and Luke 9:18–43.

Think Quietly: What did Jesus tell the Apostles about the life of his disciples? How did the experience on the mountain give them hope? How do you find hope in the midst of sadness and hard times?

Pray Together: Jesus, you are Lord. We accept our crosses and know we are following you to eternal life.

Jesus Raises Lazarus from the Dead

In the village of Bethany, not far from Jerusalem, a man became sick and died. His name was Lazarus.

Lazarus had two sisters, Mary and Martha. All three were good friends of Jesus. When Lazarus became sick, his sisters sent a message to Jesus, who was teaching in another town. They hoped he would come quickly and heal Lazarus. But that's not what happened. Jesus stayed in the other town for two more days. He said to his disciples that Lazarus's sickness would not lead to death but that it would glorify God.

Then, when Jesus finally went to see Lazarus and Mary and Martha, he told his disciples that Lazarus had fallen asleep. Do you remember how the Samaritan woman was confused when Jesus talked about living water? Do you remember Nicodemus wondering how a person could go back into his mother's body and be born again? Well, now the disciples were confused about what Jesus was saying. If Lazarus was asleep, wouldn't he just wake up? Why did Jesus need to go see him?

Jesus knew they were confused, so he told them that Lazarus had died and that it was time to go to Bethany.

When Martha heard that Jesus was coming, she went to meet him; but Mary sat at home. Martha said to Jesus, "Lord, if you had been here, my brother would not have died. [But] even now I know that whatever you ask of God, God will give you." Jesus said to her, "Your brother will rise." Martha said to him, "I know he will rise, in the resurrection on the last day." (John 11:20–24) Martha, like many Jewish people of that time, believed that all faithful people would rise from the dead at the end of time.

Jesus told her, "I am the resurrection and the life; whoever believes in me, even if he dies, will live, and everyone who lives and believes in me will never die. Do you believe this?" She said to him, "Yes, Lord. I have come to believe that you are the Messiah, the Son of God, the one who is coming into the world." (John 11:25–27)

Then Martha went to get her sister, Mary, to tell her that Jesus had arrived. When Mary saw Jesus, she reacted the same way her sister had. She told Jesus that, if he had been there, Lazarus would not have died. But she was crying as she said this, and so were

> "I am the resurrection and the life."

all the friends who were with her, coming to greet Jesus.

Jesus approached the tomb of his friend, surrounded by the weeping of those who loved him. There, Jesus could see and feel and hear all the pain around him. He could see what death did to a community. And the Scriptures say, "Jesus wept." He shared the grief of those he loved. But he also grieved the power that death had over people. The Greek word in this Scripture describes Jesus as having a deep kind of anger. He was angry that death had so much power in this world.

In those days, tombs were caves, or they were areas cut out of rock. The body of the person who had died was anointed with oils and spices and wrapped in cloths. Then it was laid in the tomb and the opening was closed with a heavy slab of stone.

Now, along with Jesus, Mary and Martha and the many friends who had come to comfort them in their grief went to the tomb where Lazarus's body was laid. Jesus told them to open the tomb. Martha reminded him that Lazarus had been dead for four days, and by now, the body would be decaying and it would stink. Jesus reminded her of their talk when he first arrived: "Did I not tell you that if you believe you will see the glory of God?" (John 11:40)

The heavy stone was moved. Jesus began to pray. He then turned to the tomb, to the space that seemed empty, quiet, and lifeless, and shouted. Yes, *shouted*.

"Lazarus, come out!" (John 11:43)

And out stumbled the man. His hands, feet, and face were still wrapped in the funeral cloths. Jesus told the crowd, "Untie him and let him go." (John 11:44)

Jesus had just demonstrated that he had more power than anything, even death. No person has that kind of power. Only God does. Only God can conquer

death, and in Bethany that day, Jesus revealed
that power.

Death has no power over Jesus, and when we are
friends with him, death and sin have no power over us,
either.

Jesus' power over evil and darkness doesn't begin
at our tombs, though. When we sin, even a little bit, we
choose death over life. Refusing to love or give or show
kindness to others gives darkness a bit more power in
our lives.

We were not made for this. We were made for light
and love!

We can think of the Sacrament of Reconciliation as
the moment when we, like Lazarus, are brought back to
life by Jesus. Jesus stands outside the little tombs we
live in—the tombs made out of selfishness, anger,
sadness, and pain. He knows we are not lost forever,
even if it seems like that to us. The worst sins and bad
habits? Jesus has power over them. Jesus doesn't want
us to live in darkness. He wants us in the light with
him, unbound—free and full of joy.

*To read the whole story in the Bible, go to John
chapter 11.*

Think Quietly: What parts of your life do you need
Jesus to raise from death? How does knowing of Jesus'
power of life and death change the way you see
the world?

Pray Together: Jesus, you are Lord of life. Come among
us and bring us out of our tombs.

Jesus Enters Jerusalem

Passover was coming, and Jesus and his friends were on the way to Jerusalem. For about three years, Jesus had walked all over the land of Israel, preaching, teaching, healing, and forgiving.

Now it was almost time for this major holy day of Passover. Jesus and his friends joined others on the way to the great city of Jerusalem. This city was the center of their faith. It was in this city where the temple stood on a hill and sacrifices were offered, day and night, in gratitude to God. Just as we like to travel to our family homes on holidays, Jewish people hoped to celebrate important feasts in their spiritual home, Jerusalem, as often as they could.

As they traveled, other pilgrims joined them on the way to Jerusalem. The faithful, the grateful, the curious, the hopeful. They all joined Jesus on the dusty, hard road, following him to Jerusalem together.

On the edges of this crowd were some people who thought Jesus was a troublemaker, someone who would harm their Jewish faith and customs. Jesus knew they were there. As he walked with his disciples, he told them what was ahead in Jerusalem. He would be arrested by the religious leaders, and they would hand him over to the Romans. He told them that, yes, he would even be killed. But, on the third day, he would rise again.

This was hard for the disciples to understand. They wondered how this could be. They swore they would be faithful. They asked if they would be with him in glory.

Jesus reminded them why he had come. "For the Son of Man did not come to be served but to serve and to give his life as a ransom for many." (Mark 10:45)

Now, before Jesus and the crowd passed through the city gate and into Jerusalem, Jesus sent two of the disciples on a mission. They went to a village close by and found a donkey that was not tied up, that was free to go with them. If anyone asked what they were doing, they would say, "The Master has need of it."

They brought the donkey to Jesus, and he sat on it. When the crowd saw this, they remembered the words of the prophet Zechariah:

> Exult greatly, O daughter Zion!
>   Shout for joy, O daughter Jerusalem!
> Behold: your king is coming to you;
>   a just savior is he,
> Humble, and riding on a donkey,
>   on a colt, the foal of a donkey. (Zechariah 9:9)

Behold: your king is coming to you, humble, and riding on a donkey.

The people cut down palm branches from the trees. They spread out their coats in front of Jesus—this was the custom when a king or hero entered a city. And the people chanted and shouted from one of their ancient prayers of joy:

> Hosanna to the Son of David;
>   blessed is he who comes in the name of
>   the Lord;
> hosanna in the highest.

And when he entered Jerusalem the whole city was shaken and asked, "Who is this?" And the crowds replied, "This is Jesus the prophet, from Nazareth in Galilee." (Matthew 21:9–11)

Why were the people cheering Jesus?

Every sign they had seen pointed to Jesus as the Messiah. For decades, the people had suffered under Roman rule. Before that, they had been ruled by other conquerors and empires on the land God had promised to them through their father Abraham. They wanted God alone to rule them.

Jesus had preached with authority. He had forgiven sins, which only God can do. He had healed the sick. And now here he was. He must be the Messiah! God had visited his people at last in a new way! It was time to praise and celebrate! The people waited in hope for a king who would free them and rule God's kingdom.

On Palm Sunday, we hear these Gospel readings and carry palm branches. As we prepare for Jesus to come among us in the Eucharist, we sing what the pilgrims with Jesus sang that day: *Blessed is he who comes in the name of the Lord! Hosanna in the highest!*

We don't take off our coats and spread them on the ground. But as we process and sing with the pilgrims around the world today and through the centuries, we are praising Jesus as our king. That means that we follow him. We trust that he loves us and knows what is best for us. We may not have coats to spread before him, but we have something better: our lives.

To read more about this in the Bible, go to Matthew 21:1–11; Mark 11:1–10; Luke 19:29–38; and John 12:12–19.

Think Quietly: Is Jesus Lord of your life? Is he the king you honor most of all?

Pray Together: Blessed is he who comes in the name of the Lord! Hosanna in the highest!

Jesus Shares a Last Supper with the Twelve

When we sit around a table and share a meal, we laugh, we joke, we listen, and maybe we argue. Love brings us together. Love spread the food that nourishes us. Love, sacrifice, bread, and cup bring us closer.

And so, one night, Jesus shared a meal with his friends. These were the twelve disciples he had chosen at the beginning of his ministry. They had traveled with him, worked with him, talked and prayed with him, and ministered to others alongside him.

This meal happened soon after Jesus arrived in Jerusalem. The city was busy with pilgrims remembering God's powerful love in the Passover festival, celebrating how he freed them from slavery in Egypt. Jesus had entered the city accompanied by some of these pilgrims. They had honored and praised him as the Son of David, as one who was coming in the name of the Lord, as the very Messiah of God.

Was real freedom at hand? Was God about to reach down and show his power again?

During this busy time, what they called the Feast of Unleavened Bread, Jesus gathered with his disciples in an upper room to celebrate. It was a time of joy, but when they had gathered for the meal, Jesus told them something shocking. "One of you will betray me." (Matthew 26:21)

This was upsetting! They wondered who would ever betray Jesus. Jesus talked to the disciples for a long time. He spoke to them about how close he was to God, and because they were close to him, that meant that they were close to God too. They were like branches and a vine. He told them that he would not be with them much longer, but they should not be afraid. When the time came that he was no longer walking with them, he would send them a helper, the Holy Spirit.

> "Take and eat; this is my body."

When it was time for Jesus to bless the bread and the wine that he was giving his friends, he said something different from what they expected.

"Take and eat; this is my body." Then he took a cup, gave thanks, and gave it to them, saying, "Drink from it, all of you, for this is my blood of the covenant, which will be shed on behalf of many for the forgiveness of sins." (Matthew 26:26–28)

Jesus did something else surprising during this meal. Because people of this time walked everywhere on dusty roads, when they entered someone's home, a servant would wash their feet.

But Jesus, their leader, knelt down and washed the disciples' dirty feet. After he finished, he said:

"If I, therefore, the master and teacher, have washed your feet, you ought to wash one another's feet. I have given you a model to follow, so that as I have done for you, you should also do." (John 13:14–15)

Peter had something else to say to Jesus during this meal. He listened to Jesus tell his friends that when he was taken and killed, they would run away. Peter told Jesus that he would never, ever run away! But Jesus answered that before the cock crowed—as roosters do when daylight comes—Peter would deny Jesus three times.

So much was happening that night, all over Jerusalem, and in that upper room.

Over at the temple, lambs were being prepared for sacrifice on the altar for the feast of freedom. Here in the upper room, Jesus was giving himself to his friends. The Lamb of God would be sacrificed for real, lasting freedom.

Throughout the city, the people were remembering God's mighty power to save. Here in the upper room, Jesus the Lord was taking the form of a slave, kneeling before his friends and washing their feet.

All over Jerusalem, food was being readied for the feast. Bread dough was being mixed, wine was being tasted and poured. The food would help people remember what God had done in that first, old covenant of love.

And here in the upper room, Jesus fed his disciples what looked like bread and wine that could only nourish the body. But as he blessed and broke it, it was transformed into something else: his body broken on the cross for them, his blood poured out. It was a New Covenant, not just for them, but for all to share. Jesus told his friends that he had been looking forward to sharing this meal with them. He had "eagerly desired" to break the bread and share the cup. The prophets had described the time of salvation as a feast. When Jesus explained to people what God's kingdom was like, he often told them it was like a banquet. And now the banquet had begun.

Jesus loves us. He eagerly desires to share his body and blood with us, to bring us into communion with him at this table, this altar.

And every time we go to Mass, that is exactly where we are. Jesus is eager to share with us, and so he brings us in to feast with him. He turns his suffering into prayer, and his prayer transforms the gifts of bread and wine into himself.

God invites us to come to the table and eat! And then God invites us to leave the table and go out to others. We can do this, now nourished by powerful, humble love. We can go do for the world what he has done for us. We can wash feet. We can feed the hungry. We can love as Jesus did!

To read more about this in the Bible, go to Matthew 26:17–30; Mark 14:12–26; Luke 22:7–39; and John 13:1—17:26.

Think Quietly: What does Jesus give us in the Last Supper? What does he want us to do with what he gives us?

Pray Together: Jesus, you are the Bread of Life. Thank you for your real presence among us.

Jesus Prays in the Garden of Gethsemane

Jesus and his friends had shared their last supper together. Jesus had washed their feet to show them that real leaders are humble and serve others. Jesus had given them the strange, sad news that one of them would betray him. And now, Jesus went to a garden to pray. All the Apostles, except for Judas, went with him.

The garden was at the bottom of the Mount of Olives, which was a hill just outside Jerusalem. The garden was called Gethsemane. Jesus and his disciples had been there before, to talk and to pray. But tonight was different.

Jesus had spoken with God's authority about the Law and the temple. He healed, worked other miracles, and forgave sins, something only God could do. And he had criticized the religious leaders quite harshly, because they were not leading the people with compassion. Then Jesus raised Lazarus from the dead, and the news of this spread very quickly. After that, some of the leaders planned to kill Jesus—and Lazarus, too!

Crowds were coming to see Jesus, outside Jerusalem but also right inside the temple, where he would preach and teach. This made the religious leaders even more upset and anxious. The people might stop listening to them and follow Jesus instead.

Jesus knew that darkness was coming, and so, after the meal, he took his friends into the garden, in the night. They sang hymns as they went, psalms of praise to God for Israel's liberation from slavery. God's people had sung these psalms for hundreds of years as they celebrated this time of Passover, of freedom.

Jesus told Peter, James, and John how sorrowful he was.

Usually, when Jesus went to pray, he went off alone, but not this time. He told some of his friends to stay where they were, but he took Peter, James, and John with him deeper into the garden. These were the same friends he had taken with him up on another mountain, where they had seen him transfigured and speaking to Moses and Elijah about his death and resurrection. And now here they were, with him again.

He told Peter, James, and John how sorrowful he was. He asked them to stay awake with him. Then he went a few yards away, lay down on the ground, and prayed, "My Father, if it is possible, let this cup pass from me; yet, not as I will, but as you will."

(Matthew 26:39)

Jesus returned to where he had left the others, and found them sleeping. They simply could not stay awake. Jesus said to them, "So you could not keep watch with me for one hour? Watch and pray that you may not undergo the test. The spirit is willing, but the flesh is weak." (Matthew 26:40–41)

Jesus went off to pray again. He was in terrible agony. In his suffering, his sweat turned to blood, and angels came to be at his side.

"My Father, if it is not possible that this cup pass without my drinking it, your will be done!" (Matthew 26:42)

Long ago, in another garden, God gave the first humans life, love, and many gifts. But they said no to God, and darkness came into the world.

But now, Jesus entered another garden and faced the darkness we humans caused by our sins. And Jesus said yes to God. He asked, that, if possible, this "cup" would pass from him—that he not go through the torture and death that waited for him. But he chose to do what God wanted, not what he wanted. And so, the garden would become a place of "yes" again.

In this very difficult time of prayer, Jesus showed us what it means to be free. We sometimes think that to be free we must follow our own ideas and desires. But Jesus showed us another way. His human will says yes to God's will. He accepts the cup. He takes it all, takes all our sin and pride, and in his loving sacrifice he transforms it, and transforms us.

On Holy Thursday night, at the end of Mass of the Last Supper, we follow him. Jesus, present in the Eucharist, is carried by the priest in procession around the church and into a special chapel. It is like we are the Apostles, following Jesus out into the Garden of Gethsemane. In fact, some churches decorate their chapels like gardens during this time, bringing in plants to surround the altar and the Eucharist.

What happens there? Deep in the night, we are invited to wait with him, to watch and to pray. Will we remain with him? Will we enter Jesus' prayer and say to our Father, *Your will be done?* Will we share the cup? Will we, through that long night with Jesus, stay awake?

To read more about this in the Bible, go to Matthew 26:36–46; Mark 14:32–42; and Luke 22:39–46.

Think Quietly: What helps me stay at Jesus' side when I am tempted to be unfaithful? How can I help others stay faithful to Jesus?

Pray Together: Jesus, we are with you in the Garden. We watch and wait with you. We love you.

Jesus Is Arrested and Put on Trial

After weeks of telling his friends that he would suffer and die in Jerusalem, Jesus shared a meal with the twelve Apostles there in the city. And he told them more shocking news: one of them would betray him. Not long after that, Judas left and went off into the night. Jesus and the others went to the Garden of Gethsemane to pray.

Now, bursting into the silence and the dark, came Judas. He had gone to the religious leaders, who had become more and more upset with Jesus. He had offered to hand Jesus over to them when the moment came, and here it was.

The crowd with Judas came with clubs and torches. Judas told the officials that he would give Jesus a kiss in greeting to show them which person to arrest. And so, with this sign of friendship, Jesus was betrayed.

Jesus said, "Judas, are you betraying the Son of Man with a kiss?" (Luke 22:48)

At this, most of Jesus' friends simply ran away. They fled into the night, except for Peter, who followed at a safe distance.

He followed as Jesus was taken, first to the Jewish religious leaders. The priests and scribes were waiting for him. They knew what Jesus was saying and doing, and they wanted to know if he was really claiming to be the Messiah, the Chosen One of God. If he claimed to be the Messiah, then this was a horrible offense against God. They brought in witnesses to testify, but they couldn't agree with one another about what Jesus had said and done. Finally, the chief priest turned to Jesus and asked him directly, "Are you the Messiah, the son of the Blessed One?" (Mark 14:61)

If Jesus said yes, he would be stoned to death, for making such a claim was blasphemy, a crime against God's holiness, the worst crime anyone could commit.

What did he say? The four Gospel writers describe this scene in different ways. But they all tell us that Jesus answered the religious leaders—in a direct way or an indirect way—that, yes, he was the Messiah. He did not deny it.

But right outside, a few yards away, Peter was denying that he was Jesus' friend.

Even though it was the middle of the night, people knew something was happening, so a crowd was outside. Peter was warming himself by a fire when a

> Most of Jesus' friends simply ran away.

woman came up and pointed to him. He had been with Jesus, she said.

Peter said no, he hadn't.

But another person insisted that, yes, Peter was one of the followers of Jesus. Peter denied it.

Yes, he was, someone else said. His accent gave him away. Peter was certainly from Galilee, and he'd been traveling with Jesus from Nazareth, who was on trial right now.

Peter got angry then, and swore. He said he didn't even know this Jesus they talked about.

And then he heard it: a rooster crowed. He remembered that Jesus had said this would happen—Peter would deny Jesus. Peter left the crowd then and went away, crying bitterly.

Back inside, the priests had heard Jesus' words and decided that he had committed the horrible sin of saying that he was the Messiah. Anyone who lied about that should be put to death. So it was time for the religious leaders to take him to the Roman official of the region, Pontius Pilate.

Pilate would not care one bit about the religious leaders' arguments about the Messiah. Pilate was a Roman who worshipped Roman gods and honored the emperor. What the Jewish people did in their own religion was of no concern to him.

It would worry him, though, if the religious leaders convinced him that Jesus was causing trouble among the people. That's what they told Pilate. Jesus was claiming to be the king of the Jews. This was causing unrest and might inspire rebellion against Rome.

Pilate questioned Jesus but could get no answers out of him. He could find no reason to condemn Jesus to death. Pilate discovered that Jesus was from Galilee, which meant that the Jewish King Herod had authority over him. So Pilate sent Jesus the prisoner to Herod.

Herod had heard about Jesus and was curious about him. Maybe Jesus would perform a miracle in front of them! But Jesus did not answer Herod's questions, at least not in a way Herod could understand.

This had happened often during Jesus' ministry. People asked Jesus questions, but their questions missed the point of who Jesus was and what his kingdom was like.

Pilate said to him, "Then you are a king?" Jesus answered, "You say I am a king. For this I was born and for this I came into the world, to testify to the truth. Everyone who belongs to the truth listens to my voice." Pilate said to him, "What is truth?" (John 18:37–38)

Jesus was taken from one authority to another. He was also stripped of his clothes and scourged, or beaten with whips. The temple guards and also the Roman soldiers mocked him. They knew he was accused of claiming to be king. So they gave him a scarlet robe, put a reed in his hand, and wove a crown made of thorns, putting it on Jesus' head. They continued to make fun of him, kneeling down in front of him and saying, "Hail, King of the Jews!"

Beaten, weak, and bleeding, Jesus was brought before the people of Jerusalem. Remember that not many days before, Jesus had entered the city with pilgrims all around him, waving palm branches and shouting, "Blessed is he!"

Now he stood before the crowds. He was bruised and beaten, still wearing his crown of thorns. Below him, in the courtyard, people watched and waited. Pilate spoke to the crowd: *Behold the Man!*

It was the tradition for the Romans to release a prisoner at Passover. Today, Pilate gave the crowd a choice. Should he release Barabbas, a rebel and murderer, or should he release this Jesus?

The cry rose from the crowd. They wanted Barabbas released.

What should be done with Jesus?
Crucify him!

To read more about this in the Bible, go to Matthew chapters 26—27; Mark chapters 14—15; Luke chapters 22—23; and John chapters 18—19.

Think Quietly: Why was Jesus arrested? Why was he a threat? How did most of Jesus' friends respond and react?

Pray Together: Jesus, you suffered for us. We are sorry for our sins.

Jesus Is Crucified and Laid in a Tomb

Jesus had spent years walking among God's people. He had walked a way of healing and forgiving, sharing God's mercy. He had walked a way of preaching and teaching the truth about God.

As he walked this way of love, he had rescued the lost, reached out to the sinners, and even raised the dead.

And now Jesus was walking through the narrow streets of Jerusalem. He was silent now, bearing on his back the heavy wood of a cross.

Jesus was still walking a way of love. It was a way of the cross—a *via crucis*.

In the Roman world, crucifixion was the punishment given to the worst criminals. The crucified person might suffer for hours or more than a day as he hung on the cross, bleeding and suffocating. It was not private suffering, either. The Romans executed people in public to scare everyone from breaking the law or going against Rome in any way.

Just like every prisoner who was crucified, Jesus carried the heavy wooden beam to where he would be executed. In this case, they planted Jesus' cross outside the city, on the hill called Golgotha. *Golgotha* means "place of the skull."

He was surrounded by crowds, but he walked alone. His friends had deserted him. Afraid of the Roman soldiers, the disciples had run away. And this time, there was no huge crowd of pilgrims shouting, "Hosanna!" and spreading palm branches in front of him.

But maybe some of the people who watched Jesus walk the way of the cross remembered the words of the prophet Isaiah:

> But he was pierced for our sins,
>   crushed for our iniquity.
> He bore the punishment that makes us whole,
>   by his wounds we were healed. (Isaiah 53:5)

Perhaps some of the people remembered the prophet's words, and remembered all that Jesus had done. Seeing him wounded like this, maybe something in their hearts told them to pay attention. They expected a Messiah to come in glory. But could this wounded Jesus be the true Messiah, coming to them in humility and suffering?

Jesus' mother, Mary, watched her son on this way of the cross. Other women stayed with her, including

> He bore the punishment that makes us whole, by his wounds we were healed.

Mary of Magdala. Also, one of the Apostles, John, was there.

Along the way, Jesus encountered other people. When he stumbled and could no longer carry his cross, the Romans ordered a man named Simon to help him.

A large crowd of people followed Jesus, including many women who mourned and lamented him. Jesus turned to them and said, "Daughters of Jerusalem, do not weep for me; weep instead for yourselves and for your children." (Luke 23:27–28)

He also encountered the other two prisoners who would be crucified with him. They arrived at Golgotha, and there Jesus and the others were nailed and tied to crosses. The crosses were raised up and placed in the ground. There Jesus and the other two prisoners hung.

Above him, the Romans nailed a sign to mock him and warn other rebels: *This is Jesus, King of the Jews*.

People standing around and watching also mocked him. They laughed at him for saying that he could destroy the temple and raise it in three days. So why was he hanging on the cross if he was so powerful? If he was the Son of God, and if he saved others, why couldn't he save himself? The words of onlookers echoed the Devil's temptation of Jesus, long ago in the desert.

Meanwhile, the soldiers divided up his clothing and gambled for it.

Even one of the criminals hanging beside Jesus mocked him. "Are you not the Messiah? Save yourself and us." (Luke 23:39)

The man on the other side of Jesus has been remembered through Church tradition as St. Dismas, a patron saint of prisoners. He scolded the other prisoner, saying that Jesus had done nothing to deserve being executed. But they, the two criminals, had been judged fairly for their crimes. Then he turned to Jesus and begged, "Jesus, remember me when you come into your kingdom." And Jesus replied, "Amen, I say to you, today you will be with me in Paradise." (Luke 23:42–43)

Jesus was crucified around noon. The Gospel writers tell us that during the hours he suffered on the cross, he spoke seven times. Through these words, he continued living the way of love.

It was a way of forgiveness. "Father, forgive them, they know not what they do." (Luke 23:34)

It was a way of community and family: "Woman, behold your son. . . . Behold your mother." (John 19:26–27)

It was a way to God's kingdom: "Amen, I say to you, today you will be with me in Paradise." (Luke 23:43)

It was a way of honesty about human suffering: "*Eloi, Eloi, lema sabachthani!* My God, my God, why have you forsaken me?" (Mark 15:34)

It was a way of seeking: "I thirst." (John 19:28)

It was a way of acceptance: "It is finished." (John 19:30)

It was a way of trust in God the Father: "Father, into your hands I commend my spirit." (Luke 23:46)

After three hours it was, indeed, finished. Jesus bowed his head, gave up his spirit, and died.

The shadows fell, clouds gathered, thunder rumbled, and the earth shook. The temple curtain, separating the holiest places from the people, split in two.

A Roman centurion stood at the foot of the cross. "Truly," he said, "this man was the Son of God!" (Mark 15:39)

Jesus' family was not from Jerusalem. They did not own a family tomb in the area, but a wealthy disciple named Joseph, from Arimathea, went to Pilate and asked for Jesus' body so that he could give it a proper burial. Mary and the others cleaned his body, anointing it with fine oils given to them by Nicodemus, the Pharisee who had visited Jesus in the night with his questions, who had been so puzzled by Jesus' words about being born again.

They wrapped Jesus' body in clean white cloths. They laid it in Joseph's new tomb, chiseled out of stone. They rolled a heavy stone in front of the entrance, sealing it. Pilate sent guards to watch the tomb.

Jesus' family and friends mourned. They searched their memories of everything Jesus had said to them. They were trying to understand what had happened and why. Jerusalem settled back to normal. It was the Sabbath. It was time to rest in the quiet.

To read more about this in the Bible, go to Matthew chapters 26—27; Mark chapters 14—15; Luke chapters 22—23; and John chapters 18—19.

Think Quietly: What are some of the ways Jesus suffered on his way of the cross? Why do all of our churches have Stations of the Cross in them, and why do we honor images of the crucified Christ?

Pray Together: Jesus, suffering Lord, help me bear my own suffering patiently and in love.

Easter

God Creates the World

In the beginning—the *genesis* of everything—there was God. Period. There was no space or time. Only God. And God was being and knowing and loving.

In the beginning, when God created the heavens and the earth . . . the earth was without form or shape, with darkness over the abyss and a mighty wind sweeping over the waters. (Genesis 1:1–2)

Then God created. He didn't have to. But freely, out of nothing, and out of love, God created.

Winds swept through darkness and over waters. God spoke, and through that word, the world came to be.

God said: Let there be light, and there was light. God saw that the light was good. God then separated the light from the darkness. God called the light "day," and the darkness he called "night." (Genesis 1:3–5)

God created the sky. He gathered the waters to make the seas, and he formed the land into continents. Then God created living things: things that would grow, breathe, reach to the light, and change. First, he created plants of all kinds, and these plants had seeds. The seeds would grow into more plants, so that plant life would keep living and growing on the earth.

Then God created lights just for this earth he had made. He created the sun to give the earth light during the day, and the moon to make a gentle glow at night. Our world would never be completely dark.

It was time for more life! So God created creatures to live in the waters: tiny fish with flickering, colorful scales and huge sea creatures who glide through the water and leap above it. He created birds of all kinds: birds who swim, swoop, and flutter, who chirp, hoot, and quack.

God created these creatures so that they could make more life. "Be fruitful and multiply," he told all the creatures. "Fill up the seas and the sky."

> God said, "Let us make human beings in our image."

The land would be full of creatures too. God created all sorts of animals: animals that walk on four legs, animals that creep, animals that crawl. They ran, hopped, and grazed. They warmed their bodies in the sunshine, they drank from the deep, cool waters, and they nestled their babies in the shade of the trees. The world would be busy, noisy, and colorful. The creatures would know how to live and what to teach their babies.

God saw all that he had made through his word. He saw the light and the darkness, the waters and the earth, the sun, moon, and stars, and all the furry, scaly, feathered creatures that filled the earth. God looked at every rock, every blade of grass, every drop of water. God saw that it was all good.

Then God decided to add one more creature to this good, good world. God said, "Let us make human beings in our image, after our likeness." (Genesis 1:26)

And there we were. Male and female, he created us.

We shared the land and water, night and day, sunshine and rain with all the other creatures. But there was one big difference: God made humans in his own image.

How could we be like God? God doesn't have a body, but we do. God has no beginning or end, but we do. God is all powerful, but our power is limited. God knows everything, but we certainly don't.

How are we made in the image of God? Well, we are free to choose what we will do or say. We can make decisions. We are free.

Also, we have the ability to create. We draw or paint or sing or build. From just an idea in our minds, we make things. We are creative.

We have minds that can think and solve problems. We are intelligent.

And we can love. We have the ability to be in relationships with one another, with God, and with the world. Not only can we love, but that's what we were created for—to love God and one another.

So when we see ourselves, we see God's image and likeness: he created us so we reflect those gifts of freedom, creativity, reason, and love.

God looked at everything he had made, and found it very good. (Genesis 1:31)

During Lent, we thought about the ways that the world—and our lives—are broken by sin. And now, during Easter, we celebrate the life that Jesus gives.

Jesus, risen from the dead, removes those limits of sin and death and brings us back to become the people God created us to be—in the beginning!

To read the whole story in the Bible, go to Genesis 1—2:2.

Think Quietly: Think about your favorite things to see and do outside. Think about your favorite animals. Think about the way you use the gifts of free will, creativity, intelligence, and love.

Pray Together: Dear God, you have created all things. We thank you for all of it. We thank you for the earth and the stars, for all the animals and all the plants. Most of all, we thank you for us. We thank you for making us in your image so that we can think, create, and love like you.

EASTER

Noah and the Flood

God made a beautiful world. And he created so many kinds of living things to grow and flourish in this world.

God even made us in his image. He gave us these gifts: the freedom to make our own choices, the creativity to sing and build and make all kinds of beauty. He gave us the gift of intelligence, minds that can think and solve problems. And he gave us the ability to love.

But, all too quickly, human beings misused those gifts. It began with our first parents, who misused the gift of freedom to disobey God. Things got worse with their sons, Cain and Abel. In a fit of anger and jealousy, Cain killed his brother. As God's Word tells us, life on earth didn't get better after that terrible sin. The beautiful world was broken. And people, whom God created to learn, love, and create, ignored their loving Creator and just did what they wanted.

People had done so much to hurt the earth and one another that God decided it was time to start over. God would give this world another chance.

There was one family that had remembered God and continued to listen to God. Noah, his wife, his sons, and their wives still listened to God and tried to live in love. This family would help God start over. God told Noah to build a huge boat—an ark—and this ark would keep them safe. Because God was about to send a great flood to wash the earth clean.

"I will bring rain down on the earth for forty days and forty nights, and so I will wipe out from the face of the earth every being that I have made." Noah complied, just as the LORD had commanded. (Genesis 7:4–5)

Noah listened to God and built the ark exactly as God told him to. He listened to God and brought animals onboard the ark: animals that walked, crawled, and flew. Noah listened and brought a male and female of every animal so that after the flood, they could have babies and life on earth could start again.

The rains came. Everywhere on earth, lakes and rivers and seas rose higher and higher. Finally, all the land was covered by water. All life on the land was wiped out by this huge flood. But Noah and his family and all the animals floated safely in the ark.

The rain stopped after forty days, but the earth was still covered. There was no dry land yet. For months and months, Noah, his family, and the animals floated until one day, God sent winds, and the waters started to go down. Noah could see just the tips of mountaintops.

After being on the ark for so long, Noah hoped they could find land again. He sent out a raven, to see if it could find a field or a tree to land in. But the raven came back because it couldn't find anything.

Then Noah sent out a dove. But it returned too, because it could find no place to land. A week later, Noah sent the dove out again. The family waited all day, and when the evening came, the dove returned. In its beak, it carried the fresh twig of an olive tree. Life was growing on earth again!

A week later, Noah let the dove go free. This time, the family waited and waited, but the dove never returned. They weren't sad, though, because this was good news. The dove had found a home on land somewhere—and perhaps they would, too!

That day, Noah peeked out of the ark and saw land. And so he, his wife, his sons, and their wives walked out of the ark and onto dry land for the first time in months. Along with them came all the animals who had lived safe and dry, protected from harm.

Noah was very thankful to God, and he wanted to tell God how grateful he was. When we are grateful to God, we pray to him and worship him, and so this is what Noah did, in the way that God's people did in those days. He built an altar and offered sacrifices on it. The smoke from the burning sacrifice rose in the air. It was a sign of Noah's thankful heart.

God had one more thing to say to Noah. God would make a promise to Noah and his children, and their children, and even *their* children. God made a covenant with Noah and the whole world. A covenant is a sacred agreement. Later, God would make a covenant with us through Abraham, through Moses, and finally through Jesus. But in this first covenant with Noah, God promised that he would never again use a flood to destroy life on earth.

"All the days of the earth,
  seedtime and harvest,
  cold and heat,
Summer and winter,
  and day and night
  shall not cease." (Genesis 8:22)

Every covenant comes with a sign. The sign of God's covenant with us through Noah is something we often see in the sky after it rains: a rainbow.

During Easter, we get a special reminder of how God always lets us start over. Just like Noah and his family, we see how God has rescued us with water. When we were baptized, God washed sin from our souls, gave us special grace, and brought us into his family and new life. The holy water we bless ourselves with when we come to church or that is sprinkled on us during Mass in the Easter season reminds us that God's help is real. That grace washes us and keeps us safe so that God's image can shine in us again, just as God intended!

To read the whole story in the Bible, go to Genesis 6:9—9:17.

Think Quietly: What bad habits keep you from living in the loving, thoughtful, and creative ways God made you to live? What are the places and times that you use holy water?

Pray Together: Lord, bless us as we turn from sin. Water us with grace so that our spirits burst with new life.

> God would give this world another chance.

God Leads His People out of Slavery in Egypt

God's people had come to Egypt when there was no food in their own land. That was many years ago, and now there were thousands of Israelites living in Egypt. Pharaoh, Egypt's leader, believed there were too many Israelites. What if they decided to take over his country? So Pharaoh began to persecute the Israelites and use them for the harshest jobs.

God heard the people's suffering and sent Moses to lead them to freedom. God had shown himself to Moses in a burning bush and revealed his name to him: I AM.

Moses wondered why God was calling him. He tried to argue with God, saying that he was not a good speaker. There was no way Moses could convince the Pharaoh to set the people free. God told Moses that his brother, Aaron, would do the talking. But Moses would be the leader. Like any of us, Moses was not perfect. But God would give him everything he needed to do God's will.

Moses and Aaron went to Pharaoh and said, "Thus says the LORD, the God of Israel: Let my people go, that they may hold a feast for me in the wilderness." Pharaoh answered, "Who is the LORD, that I should obey him and let Israel go? I do not know the LORD, and I will not let Israel go." (Exodus 5:1–2)

Moses and Aaron went to Pharaoh many times, asking for freedom. They told Pharaoh that it was God himself who was commanding this. At first this made the Pharaoh angry. Instead of giving God's people freedom, he gave them even more work to do, and he made them suffer more than before.

God sent more powerful signs. He turned Aaron's rod into a serpent in front of the court prophets and magicians. The magicians' rods turned into serpents too, but Moses's serpent ate them all! Pharaoh's heart hardened, and he would not listen to God's message through Moses.

God sent more powerful signs to Pharaoh and the people of Egypt. Through these signs, God showed his power over all the earth. In them, Pharaoh could see that everything in the world exists, moves, and breathes because of God.

The signs God sent were called plagues. Waters turned to blood. Fish died. Frogs covered the earth. Locusts swarmed all over the crops and ate them up. Animals became sick and died. People had sores on their bodies. There were hailstorms. Then, the land was covered in darkness, as though the sun would never appear again.

Every time a plague came, Pharaoh would almost agree to let God's people go. But then his heart would grow hard and stubborn again, and he said no to Moses and Aaron—no to the people, no to God.

Finally, the Lord told Moses what would happen next. In the dark of night, death would sweep through the land and kill all the firstborn. The firstborn child of every family would die, and the firstborn of all the animals would die, too.

But God's people would be protected. Each family would take a perfect lamb and slaughter it. With the lamb's blood, they would paint the doorframe of each house. And that night, they would get dressed and ready to leave. But first they would eat a meal together. They would roast the lamb, and they would make bread that could be prepared quickly. They would eat this meal standing up, with their shoes on, because they were about to go on a journey.

When death passed through Egypt that terrible night, the homes of the Israelites were protected by the blood of the lamb. Death passed over their homes, and they were safe. The people ate their meal, and they began their journey to freedom.

That was the night Pharaoh changed his mind. Death came to the Pharaoh's house and killed his firstborn son—and also the firstborn of everyone in Pharaoh's household, even the servants.

"Pharaoh arose in the night, he and all his servants and all the Egyptians; and there was loud wailing throughout Egypt, for there was not a house without its dead." (Exodus 12:30) Then Pharaoh called Moses to him and told God's people to leave.

But after the people were already on their way, Pharaoh changed his mind again. He sent his army after Moses and God's people. By this time, the Israelites had reached the Red Sea. They had to cross it to get home. The Egyptian army came up behind them, and the sea was in front of them—they were trapped! Had God led them out here just to get killed by the Egyptian army?

God told Moses to take his staff and lift it in front of the sea. As the people watched, the waters of the sea divided. Right in front of them was a path through the sea to the other side. The path was dry land, and on both sides of the path, the sea's waters held still like high, blue walls.

The people walked through the sea on this dry path and made it to the other side. Then Pharaoh's army came after them, but before the army reached the other side, the walls of water came down on top of them.

On the other side, safe at last, Moses and his sister, Miriam, led the people in a hymn of praise to God:

> "I will sing to the LORD, for he is gloriously
>   triumphant;
>   horse and chariot he has cast into the sea.
> My strength and my refuge is the LORD,
>   and he has been my savior." (Exodus 15:1–2)

They sang and celebrated, and they thanked God who had given them freedom. But they knew this was only the beginning. They still had a long journey ahead.

It was a journey that would continue for hundreds of years, this journey to true freedom. For even though the Egyptians no longer threatened them, God's people were not totally free. The people of Israel—and people all over the world—still awaited freedom from the power of sin and the darkness of death.

Who would set us free?

In time, God revealed himself again. It was Jesus, who announced that before Abraham was, "I am." Not

After being slaves in Egypt, God's people were free.

in a burning bush this time, but in the blood of the lamb and in his body shared with us: unleavened bread that feeds us on this hurried journey through life.

On the night of Holy Saturday, at the Easter Vigil, we hear this story of God's power in Egypt. This is the night of another kind of freedom. This is the night when Christ broke the prison bars of death. God's power is not defeated by anything—not by the world's powers, not by our own weakness, and not by death. God takes us through waters of Baptism on a journey from death to life. With him, we find freedom on the other side—real freedom, now and forever.

To read more of this story in the Bible, go to Exodus chapters 4—15.

Think Quietly: How did God help Moses lead the people to freedom? What does Jesus free us from?

Pray Together: God of power and mercy, lead us to true freedom.

Ezekiel and the Dry Bones

The prophet Ezekiel lived among God's people during a very discouraging time. The people had lost their hope. This was more than five hundred years before the life of Jesus. The people of Israel had grown into a large nation. God's prophets had led them, and God had sent kings to lead them, too. The kingdom of Israel became divided into two nations, the kingdom of Israel in the North and the kingdom of Judah in the South. Ezekiel lived in Judah.

Then the Babylonian Empire conquered the people of Judah. The Babylonians captured many of the people and took them back to Babylon. This is why the people of Judah were so discouraged. How could they believe that God was taking care of them now? God had let the Babylonians take them from the Promised Land. And now they were forced to live under another ruler in a foreign country.

Israel's faith in God was closely related to the land God had given them. It was a sign of being chosen; it was a sign of their covenant. How could they sing the songs of the Lord in a foreign land, there by the rivers of Babylon?

Well, the prophet Ezekiel had been taken to Babylon too, and he lived among God's people there. Because he was a prophet, he spoke to them very plainly and honestly. He reminded them of their sins. They had been unfaithful to God, and that was part of the reason they were in Babylon now. They needed to listen to God better and follow his ways.

> "Can these bones come back to life?"

One day, Ezekiel had a vision. In that vision, God took him to a valley that was covered with dried-up human bones.

God spoke to Ezekiel. "Can these bones come back to life?" "Lord GOD," [Ezekiel] answered, "you alone know that." (Ezekiel 37:3)

Then God told Ezekiel to say to the bones, "Dry bones, hear the word of the LORD!" (Ezekiel 37:4) He said to Ezekiel, "Say to these bones that the Lord gives them life."

Ezekiel did as God told him. And the bones began to move. They rattled as they came together to form skeletons. The bones were joined together, and then flesh covered the bones. And then skin covered the flesh. This was no longer a valley full of dry bones. It was a valley full of bodies that had been put back together with bone, flesh, and skin.

But something was wrong. The bodies did not move or speak. Ezekiel could see that they were not really alive. They were bodies, but they weren't living people.

We're not alive unless we're breathing. When we breathe, the air goes to every part of the body and makes everything work: the muscles and the brain and the heart. In the very first verse of the Book of Genesis, we are told that a wind from God swept over the waters as God began the work of creation. When God created the first human, he gave that human life by breathing into his nostrils.

God told Ezekiel to tell the four winds—from the east, west, north, and south—to rush down into the valley and breathe upon these bodies.

The prophet did as he was told, and wind surrounded the bodies. It filled them with breath, and they stood up. They were alive.

Then God said to Ezekiel, "These bones are the whole house of Israel. They are saying, 'Our bones are dried up, our hope is lost, and we are cut off.' Therefore, prophesy and say to them: Thus says the Lord GOD: Look! I am going to open your graves; I will make you come up out of your graves, my people, and bring you back to the land of Israel." (Ezekiel 37:11–12)

God gave Ezekiel this vision to show him that there was still hope for the people who lived in Babylon, far from their homeland. They felt discouraged, but God would give back to them the good life they longed for. They would even get to return to their homeland, although that would happen years later.

In Ezekiel's vision of a field of dry bones, God showed him what was possible. God could raise the dead. God could turn death into life. "When I open your graves and make you come up out of them, my people . . . I will put my spirit in you that you may come to life." (Ezekiel 37:13–14)

Hundreds of years after Ezekiel, people saw Jesus tortured and crucified. His body was buried in a dark tomb, and everyone expected the body to decay until only the bones were left. But then Jesus rose from the dead, and he came back to his friends—alive and breathing. They could see his wounds, and they shared a meal with him.

Jesus said, "I am the resurrection and the life," (John 11:25) and this is what it meant. For Jesus, and for all who believed, there were no fields of dry bones anymore. On the first day of the week, the first day of the new creation, God breathed life into the world again, and across the valley, we hear the prophet, we feel the breath of new life, and with him, we rise.

To read the whole story in the Bible, go to Ezekiel 37:1–14.

Think Quietly: Why did God's people lose hope? Can you think of times when you lose hope? How can Jesus give us hope in these times?

Pray Together: Lord, breathe new life into us. Give us hope.

Jesus Rises from the Dead

On a quiet morning on the first day of the week, a woman walked outside Jerusalem. She had a sad job to do. Just two days before, her friend and teacher had been unjustly killed. Fearful of the Romans, almost all his other friends and followers had run away. Only she and a few other women, including her friend's mother, remained to do what they could now. Their friend's body lay in a nearby tomb.

The woman's name was Mary of Magdala, and she was a follower of Jesus of Nazareth. He had freed Mary from seven demons who had possessed her. Jesus had given her life, and ever since that day, she had followed him, learned from him, and helped him. Today, she was going to help him again, in the only way she knew how.

The Roman official in charge of the trial and execution was named Pilate. After Jesus died, Pilate gave his body to a man named Joseph of Arimathea. Joseph owned a tomb outside the city. He told Jesus' friends and family that they could put Jesus there. In that dry, rocky part of the country, a dead body was not buried in the ground. It was laid in a stone container on top of the ground. Or it was laid inside a cave, and the cave's entrance was shut tight.

It was the custom to clean the dead body and anoint it with oils and spices, then wrap it in clean cloth. The spices would hide the odor of the body as it decayed. Mary and the other women had prepared Jesus' body for burial, but they wanted to bring more spices for it today. They were in a hurry the day Jesus died and had to leave before they were finished.

As she approached, Mary and the other women wondered how they would move the large and heavy stone that closed the entrance to the cave. But when they arrived there, they saw that the stone had already been moved.

Mary ran back to town and went to the home where the Apostles were hiding. "They have taken the Lord from the tomb, and we don't know where they put him." (John 20:2)

When Simon Peter arrived . . . he went into the tomb and saw the burial cloths there, and the cloth that had covered his head, not with the burial cloths but rolled up in a separate place. Then the other disciple also went in . . . and he saw and believed. For they did not yet understand the scripture that he had to rise from the dead. Then the disciples returned home. (John 20:6–10)

After the men went back to town, Mary stayed outside the tomb, crying. Not only was her friend and

> Mary stayed outside the tomb, crying.

teacher dead, but someone had stolen his body. She peeked inside the tomb and saw two angels in white sitting there, one at the head and one at the feet where the body of Jesus had been. And they said to her, "Woman, why are you weeping?" She said to them, "They have taken my Lord, and I don't know where they laid him." (John 20:12–13)

Then Mary turned around and saw a man standing there. He must be the gardener, who took care of the grounds around the tombs. He asked her the same question the angels had asked: why was she crying?

"Sir, if you carried him away, tell me where you laid him, and I will take him." (John 20:15)

Then the man said one word: "Mary!" When she heard him say her name, she suddenly knew who he was. Jesus!

"Teacher!" Mary cried out.

Jesus said quickly to her, "Go to my brothers and tell them, 'I am going to my Father and your Father, to my God and your God.'" (John 20:17) He told her to tell them that he was going ahead of them back to Galilee, and they would see him there. So Mary ran to the disciples right away, and told them all about it, saying, "I have seen the Lord." (John 20:18)

On the first day of creation, God spoke his word. *Let there be light!* God said. And there was light.

That morning of the first day of the week outside Jerusalem, Mary of Magdala walked in the darkness, carrying spices and oils to a dark cave, a place of the dead, quiet and full of shadows.

But Jesus had won over death and darkness. It was the first day of a new creation; it was a day in which God spoke and said again, *Let there be light!*

After the darkness of Good Friday, we rest on Holy Saturday. It is a quiet and thoughtful time. Then on

Saturday night, we gather for a vigil, which means a time of waiting. We gather after the sun has set, in the darkness, and in the darkness, a fire begins to burn.

From that fire, a single large candle is lit. Five grains of incense are embedded in the side of the candle, which help us remember the five wounds Jesus received when on the cross. On the side of the candle are written the first and last letters of the Greek alphabet, alpha and omega, because Jesus is the first and the last. In him, creation begins, and all creation is on a journey to fulfillment in him.

The paschal candle is dipped in baptismal waters, the waters in which we die and rise with Jesus. It is lit from the fire. We watch and pray in the darkness as the candle is carried through the church. We think of the darkness in our own lives: the sin, the reality of dying, and we watch the light move among us.

We hear a prayer of praise three times: *Christ our Light!* We see that glimmer of light, we think of our own darkness, and we pray in response: *Thanks be to God!*

And one by one, we each light our candles. The source of the light is that first candle, bearing the mark of Jesus' loving sacrifice.

It is God's new day. It is a new day for all of us. Jesus has broken through because he loves us. *Let there be light.*

To read the whole story in the Bible, go to John 20:1–18.

Think Quietly: Why was Mary returning to the tomb that day? How is this first day of the week like the first day of creation?

Pray Together: Risen Jesus, you have forgiven our sins and freed us from death. Alleluia!

Two Disciples on the Road to Emmaus

Two friends walked together down the road. It was morning of the first day of the week, and they were on a journey from Jerusalem to Emmaus, about seven miles away.

They had been followers of Jesus. One of them was named Cleopas. Jesus had twelve disciples who traveled with him wherever he went. But many other people followed him too. Men and women from all over the country listened to him preach and teach and came to him for help. Cleopas and his friend had watched Jesus heal the sick, forgive sinners, and tell all people, no matter who they were, that God loved them.

They knew that Jesus was a holy prophet of God. But this prophet had been arrested and crucified. The Romans had killed him as if he were a murderer or a thief. The two friends didn't understand why this had happened. This is what they were talking about on that Sunday morning as they walked.

Then a man joined them. This was not surprising, because a lot of people walked on that road. Even if they didn't know one another, they might walk together and talk for a while, just to be friendly.

The man heard the two friends discussing what had happened to Jesus, and he asked them, "What are you talking about?"

> "Were not our hearts burning within us while he spoke to us?"

They looked at him in surprise, and Cleopas said, "Are you the only visitor to Jerusalem who does not know of the things that have taken place there in these days?" And he replied to them, "What sort of things?" They said to him, "The things that happened to Jesus the Nazarene, who was a prophet mighty in deed and word before God and all the people, how our chief priests and rulers both handed him over to a sentence of death and crucified him. But we were hoping that he would be the one to redeem Israel." (Luke 24:18–21)

And something else had happened. Just that morning, the women of their group had gone to the tomb and found it empty. They couldn't find Jesus' body, but they saw angels, who told them that Jesus was alive. Then some of the men went back to the tomb and saw that it was indeed empty.

What was happening? They just didn't know. It was confusing and frightening.

The man listened to them. He then told them that if they thought about it, they would understand. "Was it not necessary that the Messiah should suffer these things and enter into his glory?" (Luke 24:26) he said.

The man continued walking with them and explained all that had been said about the Messiah, starting all the way back to Moses and the prophets.

They came to Emmaus, and the two friends invited the man to stay with them. Probably they didn't want him to walk on alone, when night was coming. He accepted their invitation. They sat down together to have a meal. Bread was part of this meal, as it always was. This man who had broken open the Scriptures for the two friends picked up the bread. He broke it to share with them, and as he did, they recognized him.

It was Jesus!

As soon as they saw who he was, he vanished, and they thought about how they had felt on their walk: "Were not our hearts burning [within us] while he spoke to us on the way and opened the scriptures to us?" (Luke 24:32)

They were so excited about this that they hurried all the way back to Jerusalem to tell the other followers of Jesus what had happened. They learned then that Jesus had appeared to Simon Peter. Everyone had news to share, and what good news it was!

―――――――

Sometimes we can be disappointed and confused. We might feel alone in the world. We might feel bad about ourselves, comparing ourselves to others and feeling as if we just aren't good enough. Maybe we've been treated unfairly.

We might be sad and worried because life is going through a big change. We might be sick, or maybe someone we love is fighting serious illness. Like Jesus' friends and disciples, we might feel empty and sad because someone we love has died.

We're walking along, trying to understand what is happening to us.

Jesus is walking with us. We might not recognize him at first, but he's there. He's our traveling companion. He broke through time and space, and just as he walked with those friends on the road to Emmaus, he walks with us, now and always.

When we go to Mass, we are like those two disciples on the road to Emmaus. They listened to the man explain God's Word, and we listen to God's Word as it is read during Mass. We hear how much God loves us. He created us, he guides us, and he entered our darkness to give us light in Jesus. It's all there in his Word at Mass. And if we listen closely, we might notice that our hearts burn with excitement, because we can hear that God speaks to us.

In the Mass, after we hear God's Word explained, we receive the Eucharist. Jesus acts through the priest to break the bread with us and for us. He's right here with us. It's no longer bread at all. It is Jesus himself, his body broken and sacrificed for our sins.

At every Mass, this is where we are: on that first Easter morning, with Jesus. He is our light, our traveling companion, and our bread. We know he's with us, and deep within us, our hearts burn with the fire of love.

To read the whole story in the Bible, go to Luke 24:13–35.

Think Quietly: What did Jesus explain to the two friends on the road? How did they finally recognize him? When we meet Jesus in the Mass, how is that like when the two disciples met Jesus on the road to Emmaus?

Pray Together: Jesus, Bread of Life, broken for us, help us see your presence among us.

The Risen Jesus Appears to His Friends

The tomb was empty. Mary of Magdala and some other women had seen this for themselves. They had told Peter and the other men, and Peter had gone to the tomb and seen that it was empty.

How could this be?

The Apostles knew Jesus had been tortured and executed. They remembered what he had told them: he would be killed in Jerusalem. He also told them he would rise from the dead. Mary of Magdala claimed that she had seen the risen Jesus.

All the Apostles could do was wait and see what would happen. They were afraid that the Romans might arrest them because they had been Jesus' followers. So, while they waited, they stayed hidden in a house with all the doors locked.

Then, into their locked room and among their fearful hearts, came Jesus.

Then, "Jesus came and stood in their midst and said to them, 'Peace be with you.'" (John 20:19)

Was this really Jesus? How did he get in? Or was this a ghost who had come through the wall?

Jesus showed them the wounds in his hands, made by the nails of crucifixion. He showed them the wound in his side, where the centurion had stabbed him with a spear. No, he was not a ghost. This wasn't a trick. He was standing there with them—they could touch him. It was truly Jesus. He had risen from the dead!

[Jesus] said to them again, "Peace be with you. As the Father has sent me, so I send you." And when he had said this, he breathed on them and said to them, "Receive the holy Spirit." (John 20:21–22)

Jesus was giving his Apostles a mission. They were to share God's mercy with others. The Holy Spirit would help them do this.

One of the Apostles was missing that night. His name was Thomas, and later, when the Apostles told him they had seen Jesus, he didn't believe them. "Unless I see the mark of the nails in his hands and put my finger into the nailmarks and put my hand into his side, I will not believe." (John 20:25)

A week later, again the Apostles were in a locked room, and again Jesus came among them and said, "Peace be with you." This time Thomas was present, so Jesus invited him to touch his wounds. Thomas recognized Jesus and said, "My Lord and my God!"

Not long after that, Simon, Thomas, James, John, and some other Apostles were at the Sea of Galilee. Peter decided to go fishing, and the others joined him. They fished all night and didn't catch anything.

As dawn approached, they saw a man standing on the shore. He called to them, asking how they had done. They told him about their bad night. He called back and told them to cast their net at the right side of the boat. Sure enough, the net was soon weighted down with fish—so heavy, they couldn't even get it into the boat!

John recognized the man. "It is the Lord!" he said, and Peter rushed through the water toward the man on the shore. It was Jesus, sitting there on the beach, bread and fish cooking on a small fire beside him.

"Have some breakfast," he said to his friends.

Later, Jesus turned to Peter and asked him a question: *Peter, do you love me?*

Jesus asked this same question three times. Each time, Peter answered that, of course, he loved Jesus. And then Jesus would say, "Feed my sheep." (John 21:17) Jesus was telling Peter to become a shepherd to the flock of believers.

When Jesus was going through his trial and torture and crucifixion, Peter denied three times that he knew Jesus. Now Jesus gave Peter the chance to say—three times—that he loved Jesus. And now Jesus gave Peter a job to do: take care of others. If anyone could reach out to the lost sheep, Peter could.

Jesus was alive. He wasn't a ghost, and he wasn't a walking corpse. He was the Jesus they had known, but they still didn't always recognize him. They could touch him. He shared meals with them—he had a body that was real. But that body could appear and disappear. This was new. Jesus was alive, but in a different way than they were. He was fully alive. He was Lord, reigning in heaven and earth.

Jesus had walked on earth for more than thirty years. When he walked on the dusty roads and through the towns and villages of Galilee, Samaria, and Judea, he spoke to people and healed them. People could hear him. They could feel his healing touch. They could talk to him. He was right there with them. He still is.

~~~~~

The Apostles experienced Jesus' risen life, and so do we. When we receive forgiveness in the Sacrament of Reconciliation from priests acting in Jesus' name, we are in that room with them and Jesus, and our sins are forgiven. He feeds us in the Eucharist. When we serve others, living out the Spiritual and Corporal Works of Mercy, we touch his wounds.

We are in Jesus, and we are called the Body of Christ, which is alive and real. Jesus is Lord of our lives—and Lord of the whole universe!

To read more about these events in the Bible, go to John 20:19–31 and John 21:1–19.

Think Quietly: How did the Apostles experience Jesus after he rose from the dead? How is this similar to how we experience Jesus in the Church today?

Pray Together: Risen Jesus, we believe in you and rejoice in the life you share with us.

> "Have some breakfast," Jesus said to his friends.

Jesus Gives the Great Commission and Ascends into Heaven

When the disciples first met Jesus, they were fishermen and tax collectors, leading ordinary lives.

Jesus had said, "Follow me," and so they had. They had followed him, listened to him, and learned from him. They had seen him heal people, share God's mercy, and reach out to the outcasts. Jesus had been arrested, tortured, and crucified. He had been laid to rest in a tomb, and in the world's eyes, that was the end of that.

But now, the disciples stood on top of a mountain in Galilee, gazing out into the big, wide world. Standing with them was Jesus himself, fully alive, because he had risen from the dead. This was real—not a dream or a vision. Matthew's Gospel says, "When they saw him, they worshiped, but they doubted." (Matthew 28:17) They knew it was Jesus, but they still didn't know what to think of all this. What would happen now?

Then Jesus answered their question:

"All power in heaven and on earth has been given to me. Go, therefore, and make disciples of all nations, baptizing them in the name of the Father, and of the Son, and of the holy Spirit, teaching them to observe all that I have commanded you. And behold, I am with you always, until the end of the age." (Matthew 28:18–20)

Jesus was Lord, not only of an earthly kingdom, not only of the land God had promised Abraham and his descendants, but of the whole world. Jesus was Lord of heaven, too. All creation had been created through him.

The whole world had to know about this! The whole world, created by God, and every person in it, lovingly brought to life by God, was being drawn back to God, the way a son or daughter is embraced by a loving father.

The world, which was lost in sin and darkness, could see the light now—the light was Jesus. But Jesus' friends had to keep telling others about him. He had taught them so much about God, and now they needed to teach others. Jesus had conquered death, too, so people did not have to be afraid anymore. Telling the Good News to everyone was the mission Jesus gave to his disciples. But they wouldn't be alone. Jesus would never abandon them.

But that's not the whole story. Sometime later, the Apostles were talking to Jesus. Remember, now Jesus

> "Go, therefore, and make disciples of all nations."

was risen from the dead. He had a real body, but he was also different. The Apostles knew this, but they still didn't understand what was happening. Jesus had said that he had power over everything, not just the nation of Israel. But the Apostles couldn't stop thinking about Israel—the land and the people and their future.

When they gathered together, they asked Jesus, "Lord, are you at this time going to restore the kingdom to Israel?" They still were hoping to get rid of the Roman government that ruled them, so that God's people could rule themselves. They were still thinking of an earthly kind of kingdom.

Jesus told them it wasn't for them to know the time of the Father's plan. All they needed to know was they were called to be his witnesses—to share with the world all they had seen him do and heard him say. And they were to be his witnesses all around the world: "You will receive power when the holy Spirit comes upon you, and you will be my witnesses in Jerusalem, throughout Judea and Samaria, and to the ends of the earth." (Acts 1:8)

When he had said this, as they were looking on, he was lifted up, and a cloud took him from their sight. (Acts 1:9)

As the Apostles stood there, searching the sky, trying to understand what had just happened, suddenly two men dressed in white garments stood beside them. They said, "Men of Galilee, why are you standing there looking at the sky? This Jesus who has been taken up from you into heaven will return in the same way as you have seen him going into heaven.'" (Acts 1:11)

What were these men saying? Jesus promised he would be with you. He did! Now stop staring above and look down instead. Look around at all the people in the world who need to hear about the healing, loving presence of Jesus. Look at all the people whose lives will be changed by the good news that Jesus lives. Look around you—and get to work!

The Apostles and other friends of Jesus, men and women, went out and told the world about Jesus. They preached. They broke bread and celebrated the Eucharist.

In the ages before the computer or even the telephone or the printing press, men and women listened carefully to the words of Jesus that the Apostles remembered. They passed on those words and wrote them down. They took these Gospels and the prayers of the Church with them, written on scrolls and in books. They carried the love of Jesus in their hearts and climbed over icy mountains, walked through dark forests, and sailed over oceans to share Jesus' words with others. Often, they had to learn other languages to do this. Sometimes, traveling to new places was dangerous and uncertain.

Jesus' friends told women, men, boys, and girls from every continent in the world this truth that would change their lives. They told them the Good News that they were here on earth because God wanted them to be here. Jesus had come to earth to forgive their sins and bring them close to God. They told them that this world is not all there is: when people say yes to God, they will live forever in God's presence. Christians traveled into jungles, villages, and cities, teaching what Jesus had taught and remembering that he was always with them.

Over the centuries, since just a few people stood on the mountain with Jesus, women, men, boys, and girls have been baptized into the Body of Christ in every corner of the world. They have heard the Great Commission and lived by it. They have passed on prayers and rituals. They have encountered Jesus in the sacraments. They have painted pictures, sculpted statues, and written music as a way of telling people about Jesus. They have taken children on their laps and, by the light of a flickering fire, guided their tiny hands across their bodies in the Sign of the Cross:

In the name of the Father, and of the Son, and of the Holy Spirit . . .

Because of them—all of them—you and I can say our prayers. Because those first friends of Jesus accepted the mission he gave them, you and I can meet Jesus in the Eucharist.

Jesus' earthly body ascended into heaven that day, but as he promised, he is always present. We don't look up at the sky. We don't have to. He is all around us: the Body of Christ.

To read the whole story in the Bible, go to Matthew 28:16–20 and Acts 1:6–11.

Think Quietly: What mission did Jesus give the Apostles? How has the Church fulfilled Jesus' Great Commission?

Pray Together: Jesus, you send us out in your name. Be with us as we spread the Good News.

EASTER

The Day of Pentecost

On that spring day in Jerusalem, the Apostles were hiding, and they were afraid.

Jesus had given his friends a mission to go out to all parts of the world, spreading the Good News. But how could they? Everyone knew they were followers of Jesus. And just a few weeks ago, a mob had turned against Jesus, and the Romans had executed him. Certainly, if they tried to go out and talk about him, they would be arrested too.

Jesus had also risen from the dead. They had seen him, eaten with him, and talked with him. He had stayed for a while and taught them. Then he left again, ascending into heaven. He promised that he would send the Holy Spirit to help them with their mission.

But when would this Spirit arrive? And what could they do now, but wait?

There they sat, gathered in a room in Jerusalem, when the air shifted. A great rush of wind spun through the entire house where Jesus' friends were. What looked like tongues of fire rested over each person's head. Then something odd happened to their own tongues. They began to speak in different languages!

Wind shakes us up and turns us around and moves us. Fire warms our cold bodies and gives us the spark of life and energy. The Holy Spirit that Jesus had promised came to the Apostles in wind and fire—moving them and giving them new energy. The Spirit drove out fear and opened up their hearts.

Jerusalem was busy that day with pilgrims celebrating Pentecost. The Jewish feast of Pentecost celebrated God's giving the Law to Moses centuries before. Although the people had synagogues in their own towns where they went to pray and study, many liked to travel to Jerusalem to celebrate big feasts such as Passover and, now, Pentecost.

Jerusalem was bustling with travelers from many different places. These travelers spoke languages from all over the world.

The Apostles had known what Jesus called them to do, but they had been afraid. No more! The Holy Spirit—the helper and Advocate that Jesus promised—now rushed in and burned out the fear. The disciples opened the doors, left the closed room behind, and plunged out into the crowds of people gathered from all over the world and started talking to them about Jesus. As they did so, the strangest thing happened. Every person heard them speak in their own language!

> Three thousand people said yes to Jesus that day and were baptized.

Now there were devout Jews from every nation under heaven staying in Jerusalem. At this sound, they gathered in a large crowd, but they were confused because each one heard them speaking in his own language. (Acts 2:5–6)

They knew that the Apostles were from Galilee, and people from Galilee spoke Aramaic. But people from out of town—who were from Libya, Egypt, Greece, and many other countries—heard these Galileans speaking their language.

In the middle of all the noise and questions, Peter stood up and began to speak. Remember when the Romans arrested Jesus, and Peter was too scared to admit that he even knew Jesus? This same Peter, who had denied Jesus three times, now spoke to the crowd with confidence. Filled with the Holy Spirit, Peter began to preach.

He told them that the prophet Joel had spoken of the days when God would pour out his Spirit, and men and women, young and old, would have visions and prophecy, and there would be signs of God's power in the heavens. That time was now, because God has sent Jesus among them.

Peter told them about the signs and wonders that Jesus had performed. He reminded them of what Jesus had suffered in their city and at their hands not long before. He told them, clearly and directly, that this Jesus they had crucified had risen from the dead—and the disciples who were gathered there had seen him with their own eyes. Everything in the history of God's people had been leading up to this:

"Therefore let the whole house of Israel know for certain that God has made him both Lord and Messiah, this Jesus whom you crucified." (Acts 2:36)

The people listening were struck deeply by Peter's words. It was shocking, life-changing news that all God's people had been waiting for. The Messiah had come, and it was Jesus of Nazareth, risen from the dead. What should they do?

"Repent and be baptized, every one of you, in the name of Jesus Christ for the forgiveness of your sins; and you will receive the gift of the holy Spirit." (Acts 2:38)

Luke, the writer of the Acts of the Apostles, tells us that three thousand people said yes to life with Jesus that day and were baptized. This was the beginning of the Church!

Jesus sends us the Holy Spirit, too. When we celebrate the Sacrament of Confirmation, we receive the gifts of the Spirit, just as the Apostles did. The bishop and priests, wearing red to stand for the Holy Spirit, lay their hands on us in prayer and anoint us with chrism, the holy oil that seals us with the Spirit that Jesus promised. Open to that Spirit, we grow in those same gifts that the Apostles received. We are filled with the Spirit that Jesus sends us because he loves us. With this Holy Spirit alive in us, we trust God, we take a deep breath, and we go out into the busy streets to tell others about Jesus.

To read the whole story in the Bible, go to Acts chapter 2.

Think Quietly: How did the Holy Spirit change the Apostles' lives? What were they able to do as a result? How does the Holy Spirit come to us today?

Pray Together: Come, Holy Spirit, fill the hearts of your people, and warm our hearts with the fire of your love!

Stephen Dies for His Faith

In Jerusalem, the Christian community was growing.

It had been just a few years since the coming of the Holy Spirit at Pentecost. The followers of Jesus shared the Eucharist together every week. They shared food and clothing and other goods with one another. They helped the poor and the sick. And they kept spreading the Good News about Jesus.

It can be hard to stay organized when your group grows, especially when different kinds of people start joining. Most of the followers of Jesus were Jewish. They knew that Jesus was the Messiah, the Chosen

One of God. They were Jewish people who believed that the Messiah had come.

But even among the Jewish people, there were differences. Most of the people living in the land of Israel spoke a language called Aramaic and read the Scriptures and worshipped in Hebrew. But outside of Israel, there were many Jewish people who spoke Greek as their language and read a Greek translation of God's Word. These Greek-speaking Jewish people were called Hellenists.

Hellenists were starting to follow Jesus too, and one day the Hellenists complained to the Christian leaders. The widows of their group were being left out when Jesus' followers gave out food to the needy, which they did every day.

The Christian leaders wanted to make sure that the people who were preaching and teaching out in the community had time to do that. They couldn't preach and teach and also be in charge of feeding everyone. So they prayed and then selected seven men who would make certain that the people who needed help would get it.

The group of leaders laid their hands on these men to show that they were chosen for this service in the Christian community. We think of these men as the first deacons of the Church. Today, when deacons and priests receive the Sacrament of Holy Orders, the bishop and any priest present lays his hands on the head of each person being ordained. In that moment, that person receives the Holy Spirit in a special way—just as those first deacons did.

One of these men was named Stephen. Stephen helped the needy, but he was also a powerful preacher. Through Stephen's prayer and faith, God performed signs and miracles. This started upsetting and worrying some religious leaders. They stirred up anger against Stephen and got false witnesses to say that he had been speaking against the temple and saying that Jesus would destroy it.

So Stephen was brought to the council of religious leaders to explain himself. But he didn't just explain his own words and actions. Stephen went through the whole history of God's people, beginning with Abraham and ending with Jesus.

He told all the stories of God's power and mercy. He also reminded those listening of how God's people had often complained and rebelled. God had given them leaders and prophets, but many times the people ignored them and even turned away from God. This was the pattern in the past, Stephen said, and this was still the pattern today. That's why Jesus, the Messiah, had been crucified.

What Stephen had to say was shocking and brave. He faced the religious leaders and said, "You stiff-necked people . . . you always oppose the holy Spirit; you are just like your ancestors. Which of the prophets did your ancestors not persecute? They put to death those who foretold the coming of the righteous one, whose betrayers and murderers you have now become. You received the law as transmitted by angels, but you did not observe it." (Acts 7:51–53)

This was too much! Stephen was accusing the religious leaders of being deeply unfaithful to God. Their anger grew. Stephen looked up and saw a vision of heaven, where Jesus stood at the right hand of God.

The "right hand of God" was a symbolic way of describing God's power. Stephen was saying that Jesus, whom their council had handed over to the Romans for execution, was alive with the Father and sharing his power. To the religious leaders, this was blasphemy and an insult to God.

So the council took Stephen outside the city. They began to throw stones at him. But first they took off their coats. While they stoned Stephen, a young man named Saul held their coats for them.

Before he died, Stephen prayed twice. Knowing that he would die, he prayed, "Lord Jesus, receive my spirit." (Acts 7:59) Then he prayed, "Lord, do not hold this sin against them." (Acts 7:60)

Does that sound familiar? Jesus said the same things as he was dying on the cross. Stephen was in close communion with Jesus, even as he died.

Stephen was the first Christian to die for his faith. Such a person is called a *martyr*, which means "witness." Stephen died faithful to Jesus. He kept speaking as a witness to what Jesus had said and done. And Stephen shared the mercy and forgiveness of Jesus with those who needed it most.

> Stephen looked up and saw Jesus in heaven, at the right hand of God.

If we are following Jesus and are living like him, then there may be a cross. We bear small crosses of hurt feelings—and heavy ones of sickness and pain. We may meet people who think we are wrong for loving Jesus. That's a heavy cross. How can we bear it?

Stephen shows us the way. We don't seek a cross, but if it comes to us, we don't run from it either. We keep Jesus at the center of our hearts, remembering that our journey keeps going to eternity, no matter what obstacles the world puts in our way.

To read the whole story, including all of Stephen's speech before the religious leaders, go to Acts chapters 6—7.

Think Quietly: How was Stephen's martyrdom like Jesus' death?

Pray Together: Lord, give us the strength to be faithful to you always. St. Stephen, pray for us!

Healing at the Beautiful Gate

All day, every day, worshippers and pilgrims walked through the temple gate. And every day, a man lying on a mat watched them.

This man had never been able to walk at all. Because he could not work, his friends and family brought him to this same spot every day, where he would beg. Would someone share a coin or a scrap of food?

The two men approaching the temple that afternoon looked like all the other people passing by. But they were Peter and James, Jesus' friends, and they were on their way to the temple to pray. This was a few weeks after Jesus' Ascension and after his followers had received the Holy Spirit at Pentecost. The Christian community was growing. They were learning more about Jesus, reflecting on all he had taught them. They were preaching and baptizing. They were meeting Jesus in their sharing of the Eucharist.

Jesus was not with them in that earthly way anymore, but he was still with them in these weeks after the first Easter. He was with them because they *were* the Body of Christ on earth now. They were his voice, preaching and teaching. And they shared Jesus' compassion as they helped the poorest among them.

Now Peter and James stood with this man, ill since birth and never able to take a step. Jesus had told his friends to share the Good News and to help bring the world back into close relationship with God the Father. And here they were, part of the living Body of Christ on earth now. And here was this man, who needed to be healed.

They couldn't keep this Good News to themselves!

When he saw Peter and John about to go into the temple, he asked for alms. But Peter looked intently at him, as did John, and said, "Look at us." He paid attention to them, expecting to receive something from them. Peter said, "I have neither silver nor gold, but what I do have I give you: in the name of Jesus Christ the Nazorean, [rise and] walk." Then Peter took him by the right hand and raised him up, and immediately his feet and ankles grew strong. He leaped up, stood, and walked around, and went into the temple with them, walking and jumping and praising God. (Acts 3:3–8)

This man had begged at that door of the temple for years, and everyone recognized him. He had never walked in all the years they had known him. And now he was not only walking but also jumping around! What was going on here? People were full of questions, so Peter decided to use this opportunity to tell them more.

He reminded the crowd of all that God had done for his people through history. He told them that the prophets had foretold the coming of the Messiah, and that Jesus of Nazareth was this Messiah. But he had been killed not long ago by their leaders. Then he had risen from the dead. And it was through this Jesus, risen and alive in a new way, that this man could walk.

By this time, a crowd had gathered to listen to Peter. Everyone was talking about a man being healed. It was no surprise that the religious leaders found out and came to see what was happening.

The priests, the captain of the temple guard, and the Sadducees confronted them, disturbed that they were teaching the people and proclaiming in Jesus the resurrection of the dead. They laid hands on them and put them in custody. (Acts 4:1–3)

Peter had run away when Jesus was crucified. He had made mistakes, failed, sinned. But he had also been forgiven and filled with the power of the Holy Spirit at Pentecost. He was no longer afraid. There, in front of the very same religious leaders who had condemned Jesus to the cross, Peter spoke boldly. Jesus was Lord, and in him, God was working to heal this broken, sad world.

So Peter spoke to the religious leaders. He told them outright, "This man is standing before you in good health in the name of Jesus Christ the Nazorean whom you crucified, whom God raised from the dead; in his name this man stands before you healed." This Jesus "is 'the stone rejected by you, the builders, which has become the cornerstone.'" (Acts 4:10–11)

This was a complicated situation for the religious leaders. They were astonished at Peter's words, for they knew that this man was just a fisherman and not, like them, educated in the Law. They wanted to make Jesus' disciples stop preaching, but they didn't want to make the crowds angry, either.

So they just let Peter and James go free. But they told them not to talk about Jesus.

Well, Peter told them, they weren't going to stop talking about what they had seen and heard for themselves. This is what they had seen and heard: Jesus the Lord, risen and still alive, acting in the world. They couldn't stay quiet about this.

When Peter and James returned to the rest of Jesus' followers, they reported what had happened, and the whole group prayed. They didn't pray for safety. They didn't pray for an end to persecution. They didn't even pray for protection.

They prayed for the strength to speak boldly and for the Lord to keep healing in Jesus' name. And again, the room shook with the power of the Holy Spirit, just as it had at Pentecost.

In these weeks after Easter, during Mass, we hear these stories from the Acts of the Apostles. It's as if the story has never been interrupted since those exciting first days. Through *our* hands, Jesus still helps people in need. He preaches and teaches through the Church, and he feeds us through the Eucharist.

It doesn't matter how old we are. We may have "neither silver nor gold," but we have Jesus' love, and the world still waits for that gift!

To read about these events in the Bible, go to Acts chapters 3—4.

Think Quietly: What did Peter and James have to give the man at the temple gate? How is what Christians do today similar to the way these early Christians lived?

Pray Together: Holy Spirit, help us be strong and brave as we share the Good News.

The Conversion of Paul

We would expect Peter and John and the other Apostles to be leaders for the early Christians. They had lived with Jesus and traveled with him. They had learned from him and been his friends.

But God was preparing another man to join them in leading the Church. And he was not a man you would expect to help Jesus' followers.

Saul was born in Tarsus, which is in the country we now call Turkey. He was Jewish, and he studied under the great rabbi Gamaliel and became a scholar of the Jewish faith. He loved his faith so much that he defended it against any enemies who would try to change it. Well, Jesus had brought a big change—he was the Messiah! But many of the Jews did not accept this, and Saul was one of them. He thought that Jesus and his followers were ruining the Jewish faith. So Saul worked hard against the early Christians. He would question them about their beliefs, and he wanted to arrest them so they would stop spreading stories about Jesus the Messiah.

In fact, Saul was at the execution of the first Christian martyr, Stephen. Saul was the young man who guarded the coats of those who stoned Stephen to death.

Years later, Saul was trying to get rid of more Christians. More and more people were believing that this Jesus was the Messiah and were following him. The movement—the followers of "the Way"—was spreading outside Jerusalem, even all the way to Damascus in the country we now call Syria.

The Jerusalem leaders gave Saul letters to take to the synagogues in Damascus. These letters stated that Saul had the authority to find followers of the Way and bring them back to Jerusalem for questioning.

On his journey, as he was nearing Damascus, a light from the sky suddenly flashed around him. He fell to the ground and heard a voice saying to him, "Saul, Saul, why are you persecuting me?" Saul said, "Who are you, sir?" The reply came, "I am Jesus, whom you are persecuting. Now get up and go into the city and you will be told what you must do." (Acts 9:3–6)

Saul's companions saw the light, but they didn't hear the voice, and they had no idea what was happening. Saul stood up, but he was still blinded from the bright light, so his companions had to lead him by the hand into the city.

After three days, a man named Ananias found Saul. Ananias had seen a vision while he was praying. And in the vision, God told him to go find the man named Saul. Ananias wondered if that was a good idea.

> Saul was trying to get rid of more Christians.

All the Christians had heard of Saul. He had a reputation for persecuting Jesus' followers. They had also heard that Saul was in Damascus, hunting for more Christians.

But God assured Ananias that he had a plan for Saul.

Ananias indeed found Saul and laid his hands upon him, and at that moment, after three days of blindness, Saul could see again. After living in darkness, Saul was in the light.

Saul was baptized, and he stayed with the Christians in Damascus for a while, learning more about Jesus.

Why had this happened? Why had Jesus come to Saul in such a way? What was Saul supposed to do now?

God had a specific mission for Saul: he would bring the Good News of Jesus to the Gentiles. Gentiles were people who were not Jewish and who followed the religions of Rome, Greece, and other nations of the world. Jesus' earliest followers were Jewish, and they understood Jesus as Lord and Messiah of the Jewish people. They knew that he came to save all people, but it was hard for them to see how this would happen. Wouldn't any follower of Jesus need to accept and practice the laws and beliefs of God's people, the Jews?

What a surprise—God chose an expert teacher of the Jewish faith to take the Good News of Jesus to people outside the Jewish faith. Saul was a teacher of the Law and an enemy of Christians, but God set him on a whole new path. How unlikely, but how true, and what a strong sign of hope!

The Jewish form of Saul's name was *Saul*. But he was also a Roman citizen, and the Roman form of his name was *Paul*. After he started his missionary work with the Gentiles, he used *Paul* all the time. It was a sign of his mission to take the gospel to people everywhere.

Paul spent the rest of his life traveling what he knew as the whole world. Taking other Christian companions with him, he went on three missionary journeys. He preached in the synagogues and public places. He was attacked, arrested, and imprisoned. He was even shipwrecked.

Along the way, Paul wrote letters—lots of letters. These letters, called epistles, were written to the Christian communities that Paul had helped on his journeys: Christians in Corinth, in Galatia, in Philippi, and even in Rome. Paul's last journey was to Rome. But this time he was taken in chains, under arrest for his missionary work. He would stay in prison for some time and then be executed. Paul, who had been an enemy of Jesus, became one of the early martyrs of the Christian faith.

It was the last step in a life that shows how God can use any of us to share the Good News. God uses our strengths—and Paul had many—and turns them to good.

In God's eyes, no one is beyond hope!

To read the whole story in the Bible, go to Acts 9:1–19.

Think Quietly: Why was Paul a surprising person to become a great friend of Jesus? How did God use Paul to tell the world about Jesus?

Pray Together: Lord, may we be strong witnesses to truth. St. Paul, pray for us!

The Life of the Early Christians

All kinds of people had heard the Good News about Jesus: women and men, young and old, from all sorts of countries and speaking different languages. They heard what the Apostles preached about Jesus. He had been sent by God, he had suffered a terrible death, and he had risen from the dead and now sat at the right hand of the Father.

They heard this Good News, and they wanted to follow Jesus. What should they do now?

When Peter preached to the crowds at Pentecost, he told them how to begin: repent of their sins and be baptized. Go down into the waters, just as Jesus had descended into the darkness of the tomb. Then rise again with him into new life!

But what did this new life look like? People still had to live their ordinary lives. They took care of their children, went to work, cooked meals, and talked with friends. In their new life with Jesus, what would change? And what would stay the same?

In the Acts of the Apostles, we learn a little bit about the lives of the early Christians, mostly in the city of Jerusalem. The earliest followers of Jesus were Jews, and so they continued to worship in the temple and to pray the same prayers that all Jewish people prayed.

But they did something else, too. Every week, they gathered in their homes, and they "broke bread"—they shared a meal together. This meal was like the Last Supper the disciples had with Jesus. The Christians shared the bread and wine, which had become Jesus' body and blood. They celebrated the Eucharist, as Jesus had told them. At the Last Supper, he said, "Do this in memory of me."

But what else had Jesus said? What else had he told his Apostles that they now were telling others?

Jesus told his friends that when they loved and served those in need, they were serving him. So this is what the first Christians did:

All who believed were together and had all things in common; they would sell their property and possessions and divide them among all according to each one's need. . . . There was no needy person among them, for those who owned property or houses would sell them, bring the proceeds of the sale, and put them at the feet of the apostles, and they were distributed to each according to need. (Acts 2:44–45; Acts 4:34–35)

Jesus told his Apostles to spread the Good News of God's mercy, and so they preached to people and healed them. Jesus told them they would be persecuted for telling the truth about him, and they were. These early Christians were mistreated and even put in prison for speaking about Jesus.

Jesus had told the Apostles to lead the people. With the help of the Holy Spirit, leaders such as Peter and Barnabas taught the new Christians. All together they prayed, they took care of one another, and they shared God's love with all who would listen. The whole community of new Christians listened to God. Their community grew and grew.

One day, Peter visited a friend in a town called Joppa. He went on the flat roof of the house to pray. And while he was praying, he had a vision of a sheet being lowered from the heavens. This sheet was filled with all different kinds of animals. A voice told Peter to eat. Peter responded that some of those animals were unclean, and he had always obeyed the Law and never eaten an unclean animal. The voice said, "What God has made clean, you are not to call profane." This happened three times. (Acts 10:15–16)

Peter had no idea what this meant. While he was thinking about these strange instructions, two men came to his house. They said that their master, a Roman commander named Cornelius, had seen Peter in a dream and sent them to find him.

Cornelius was a Roman, and he was a Gentile—not a Jew. According to Jewish law, a Jew could not enter the house of a Gentile. Gentiles were "unclean" because they did not obey all the laws of God's people. But then Peter remembered his vision. He remembered God telling him that he must not call something unclean if God called it clean.

Peter went to Cornelius's home in Caesarea. Cornelius wasn't Jewish, but he had always honored God in the best way he knew. He told Peter about his dream.

Then Peter said, "In truth, I see that God shows no partiality. Rather, in every nation whoever fears him and acts uprightly is acceptable to him." (Acts 10:34–35) Now Peter understood why God had brought them together. Peter told Cornelius about Jesus. Cornelius and his entire household opened their hearts to Jesus, the Spirit filled their lives, and Peter baptized them. Peter understood now that God's love was meant for all people, not just Jews. God had brought Cornelius to faith in Jesus. God wanted to draw all people to his love and care.

More and more Gentiles became followers of Jesus. This was good news, but it was also a problem. These Gentiles—such as Cornelius and his family—did not know the laws God had given to the Israelites. Now that they were followers of Jesus, should they become Jewish and follow the Jewish laws too? The Apostles didn't know what to think about this.

This became such a big question that the church leaders, including Peter, Barnabas, Paul, and others, came together for a big meeting in Jerusalem. They prayed. They talked. They argued. Then they prayed and talked some more. Finally, led by the Holy Spirit, they came to a decision. If you wanted to follow Jesus and be baptized, you did not also have to become Jewish. Jesus had opened the doors of God's love to all people. Through listening and letting the Spirit guide them, the first Christians grew in their understanding of God's will.

> Peter understood now that God's love was meant for all people.

The Body of Christ on earth today has grown a lot since those early days. But are we that different? We still live as witnesses to Jesus. We still preach and teach and try to share the healing mercy of Jesus and the Good News of eternal life. We still have to grow and change as a Church. We still bring healing to the suffering. We still share what we have. Church leaders still gather to make decisions. And in some parts of the world, Christians are still persecuted. There are still Christians who live in community and share what they have in common. Men and women who live in religious communities as brothers, priests, and sisters live in this way.

And just like the early Christians, we do as Jesus said. In memory of him, we break the bread and eat it, and we drink the wine. We take care of one another and try to love as Jesus loves. We share love and life across space, across time, one in Him, one in the Body of Christ.

To read about these events in the Bible, go to Acts 2:42–47; Acts 4:32–37; Acts 10:1—11:18; Acts 15.

Think Quietly: Think about your daily life and the lives of others in your Church. How are you trying to live like Jesus?

Pray Together: Holy Spirit, show us how to live together in love, the way Jesus loves all of us.

About the Author

Amy Welborn is the author of *Loyola Kids Book of Saints* and *Loyola Kids Book of Heroes*. A former catechetical leader, she has a passion for helping children understand their faith at a deeper level and for helping them live their faith with confidence and joy. Her Web site is www.amywelborn.com.

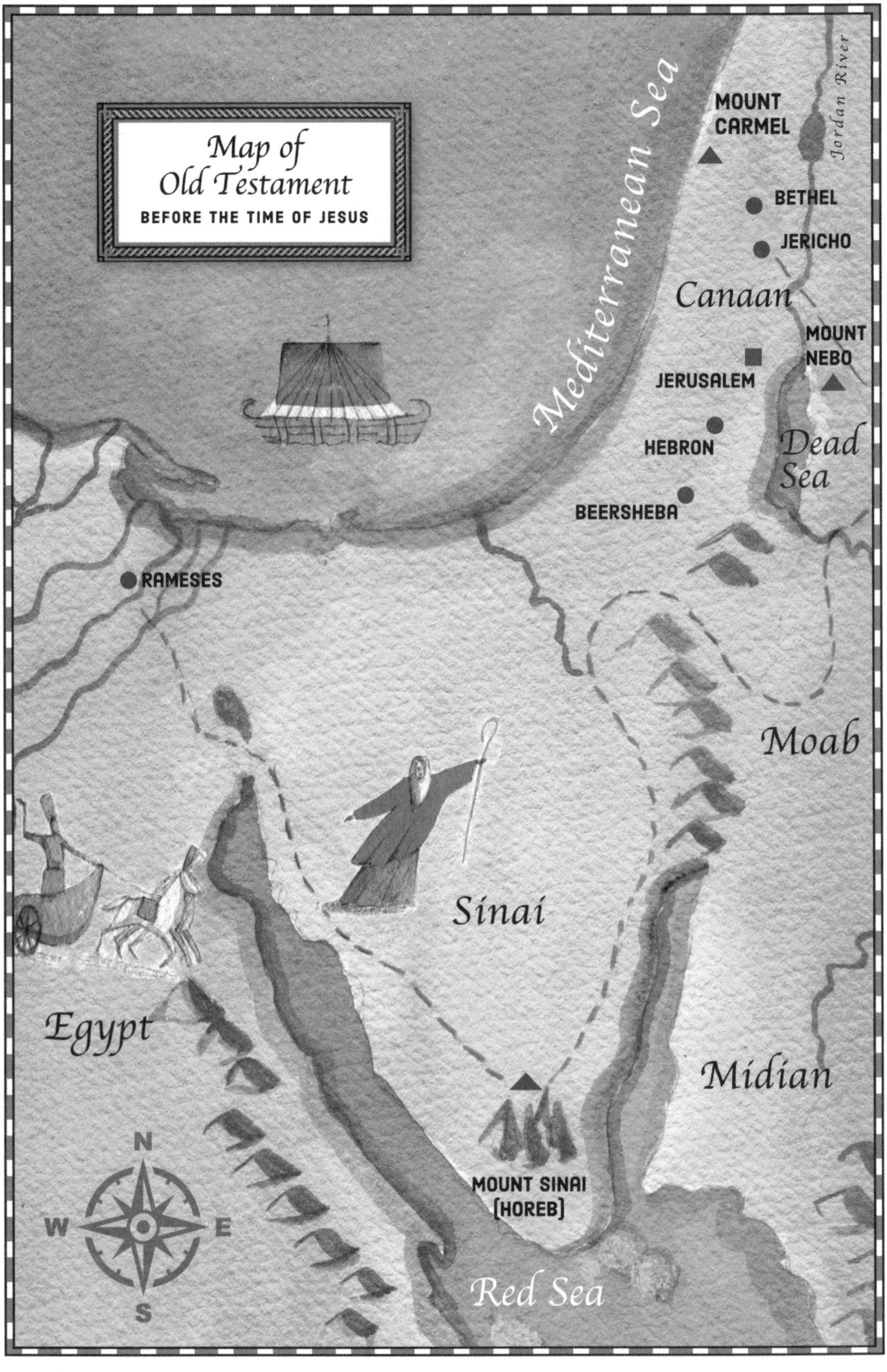

Map of
Old Testament
BEFORE THE TIME OF JESUS

Mediterranean Sea

Jordan River

MOUNT CARMEL

BETHEL

JERICHO

Canaan

MOUNT NEBO

JERUSALEM

Dead Sea

HEBRON

BEERSHEBA

RAMESES

Moab

Sinai

Egypt

Midian

MOUNT SINAI [HOREB]

Red Sea

N W E S